New Directions for Student Services

John H. Schuh
EDITOR-IN-CHIEF

Elizabeth J. Whitt
ASSOCIATE EDITOR

Serving the Millennial Generation

Michael D. Coomes
Robert DeBard
EDITORS

Number 106 • Summer 2004
Jossey-Bass
San Francisco

SERVING THE MILLENNIAL GENERATION
Michael D. Coomes, Robert DeBard (eds.)
New Directions for Student Services, no. 106
John H. Schuh, Editor-in-Chief
Elizabeth J. Whitt, Associate Editor

NEW DIRECTIONS FOR STUDENT SERVICES (ISSN 0164-7970, e-ISSN 1536-0695) is part of The Jossey-Bass Higher and Adult Education Series and is published quarterly by Wiley Subscription Services, Inc., A Wiley Company, at Jossey-Bass, 989 Market Street, San Francisco, California 94103-1741. Periodicals Postage Paid at San Francisco, California, and at additional mailing offices. POSTMASTER: Send address changes to New Directions for Student Services, Jossey-Bass, 989 Market Street, San Francisco, California 94103-1741.

New Directions for Student Services is indexed in College Student Personnel Abstracts and Contents Pages in Education.

Microfilm copies of issues and articles are available in 16mm and 35mm, as well as microfiche in 105mm, through University Microfilms Inc., 300 North Zeeb Road, Ann Arbor, Michigan 48106-1346.

SUBSCRIPTIONS cost $75.00 for individuals and $160.00 for institutions, agencies, and libraries. See ordering information page at end of book.

EDITORIAL CORRESPONDENCE should be sent to the Editor-in-Chief, John H. Schuh, N 243 Lagomarcino Hall, Iowa State University, Ames, Iowa 50011

Jossey-Bass Web address: www.josseybass.com

CONTENTS

EDITORS' NOTES

> Time flows in many ways, but two modes stand out for their
> prominence in nature and their symbolic role in making lives
> intelligible.
>
> Time includes *arrows* of direction that tell stories in distinct
> stages, causally linked—birth to death, rags to riches.
>
> Time also flows in *cycles* of repetition that locate a necessary sta-
> bility amid the confusion of life—days, years, generations.
> —Gould, 2003, p. 54

As Gould aptly points out, humans have a need for both arrows and cycles.
The arrows of time allow us to "forge time into stories," and the cycles of
time "grant stability, predictability and place" (2003, p. 55). The purpose of
this *New Directions* sourcebook is to explore the cycle of generations as a
source of insight for making the lives of our students intelligible to student
affairs personnel who will serve members of this emerging new generation.

Higher education is on the cusp of a new enrollment boom. It is estimated that by 2012 total college enrollment will exceed 15.8 million students, an increase of more than 12 percent over 2003 enrollment levels (U.S.
Department of Education, 2002). The bulk of this increase will consist of
traditional age students who are members of the Millennial generation. This
generation of students and their attitudes, beliefs, and behaviors will require
student affairs practitioners to adopt new learning and service strategies,
rethink student development theories, and modify educational environments. It is the goal of this *New Directions* sourcebook to give readers a
foundation for understanding this newest generation of students and to offer
suggestions on how to educate and serve them effectively.

In Chapter One, the editors present an overview of a generational
model for understanding and working with college students. This founda-
tional chapter lays the groundwork for understanding generations and provides a demographic snapshot of the four generations of students, faculty,
and administrators who make up the bulk of today's college population.

Chapter Two, by Michael D. Coomes, builds on the foundation laid in
Chapter One. Coomes suggests that an understanding of the recurrent patterns of history and the influences of culture, especially popular culture, is
an important tool for analyzing and appreciating generations. In addition to
schemes for understanding and interpreting history and popular culture,
the author suggests a set of historical and popular culture trends that are
shaping the lives of the Millennial generation.

Robert DeBard uses the information presented in the first two chapters to develop a portrait of the Millennial generation in Chapter Three. A readily agreed upon set of generational characteristics have been developed to explain the Millennial generation (Strauss and Howe, 1991). DeBard discusses these characteristics and contrasts them with the generational characteristics of members of Generation X and the Baby Boom generation to explore how the values maintained by each generation can both hinder and enhance our work with students.

Student development has been the primary theoretical and philosophical foundation for student affairs work since the 1970s (Strange, 1994). In Chapter Four, C. Carney Strange uses the Millennial characteristics presented in Chapter Three to examine our existing theories of student development. In addition to presenting an overview of extant student development theories, Strange suggests how those theories may have to be expanded to account for the unique characteristics of Millennial students.

The primary mission of the university is to foster learning. Using the *Seven Principles of Good Practice in Undergraduate Education* (Chickering and Gamson, 1987), Maureen E. Wilson discusses how to foster learning for Millennial students in Chapter Five. Wilson discusses how to set high expectations for students, involve parents in the learning experience, employ new learning technologies, and meet the special learning needs of students with disabilities.

A defining characteristic of members of the Millennial generation is their diversity. Ellen M. Broido, the author of Chapter Six, presents a detailed examination of that diversity in all its richness (for example, race, sexual identity, political orientation). After detailing the extent of diversity within the Millennial generation, Broido discusses how educators can capitalize on that diversity to foster social justice in the college environment.

John Wesley Lowery concludes the sourcebook with a discussion of how to effectively serve Millennial students in Chapter Seven. Lowery examines how the characteristics of Millennial students require student affairs educators to rethink how they offer learning opportunities, deliver services, and organize their work. Special attention is paid to how student affairs educators can use technology to reach students who are looking for easily accessible, round-the-clock service.

Creating understanding, fostering learning, developing a thirst for social justice, and providing effective services are not new goals for the student affairs profession. What is new is the student cohort that student affairs educators will be asked to guide during the next twenty years. This generation of confident, sheltered, and conventional young adults (Howe and Strauss, 2000) offers student affairs professionals unique educational opportunities. For many midlevel and senior student affairs officers, members of the Millennial generation represent the last generation they will work with in their role as educators. As such, the education of this generation presents a unique imperative for guidance. Generations of youth are formed by exploring the values of their elders, accepting some and rejecting others. By clearly articulating their values, by socializing new students to the values of the academy, and by remaining true to the values of the student affairs profession, Baby Boomer and Generation X faculty, administrators, and staff have the opportunity to help shape the values of Millennials and the future of the nation.

References

Chickering, A. W., and Gamson, Z. F. "Seven Principles for Good Practice in Undergraduate Education." *AAHE Bulletin*, 1987, *39*(7), 3–7.

Gould, S. J. *Triumph and Tragedy in Mudville: A Lifelong Passion for Baseball.* New York: Norton, 2003.

Howe, N., and Strauss, W. *Millennials Rising: The Next Great Generation.* New York: Vintage Books, 2000.

Strange, C. "Student Development: The Evolution and Status of an Essential Idea." *Journal of College Student Development*, 1994, *35*(6), 399–412.

Strauss, W., and Howe, N. *Generations: The History of America'sFuture, 1584 to 2069.* New York: Morrow, 1991.

U.S. Department of Education. *Projections of Education Statistics to 2012* (31st ed.). Washington, D.C.: U.S. Department of Education, 2002.

MICHAEL D. COOMES *is associate professor of higher education and student affairs at Bowling Green State University in Ohio. He is the editor of* The Role Student Aid Plays in Enrollment Management *and coeditor of* Student Services in a Changing Federal Climate *in the New Directions for Student Services series.*

ROBERT DEBARD *is associate professor of higher education and student affairs at Bowling Green State University, where he also serves as the interim director of the School of Leadership and Policy Studies. Author of* Getting Results: A Guide to Managing Resources in Student Affairs, *he was formerly the dean and campus executive officer of Firelands College of Bowling Green State University.*

1

This chapter establishes the conceptual framework for understanding the Millennial generation by presenting a theoretical model of generational succession that demonstrates the value of studying how the values of one generation interact with and are influenced by others.

A Generational Approach to Understanding Students

Michael D. Coomes, Robert DeBard

Faculty and staff working within institutions of higher education place confidence in the future through the development of college students because they have such a vested interest in their growth and development. This sense of optimism is particularly important to student affairs practitioners since the intentional outcomes of this profession have less to do with objective performance than with the more amorphous development of valued behaviors (Astin, 1995). These valued behaviors are determined through a combination of internal drive and external pressure that makes up the motivation of college students. Creating the perception that growth is positively affected by what happens in college is necessary for students and those who would sponsor their attendance. Obviously, this perception must become a demonstrated reality if intentional outcomes are to be achieved during the collegiate experience and this positive perspective is to be maintained for the future (Pascarella and Terenzini, 1991).

This chapter presents a discussion of the efficacy of a generational model for understanding students (and those who work with them). A framework for understanding generations is reviewed in order to establish a template within which the Millennial generation can be placed. Finally, this introductory chapter concludes with basic demographic information about the various generations currently to be found on college campuses.

Understanding Individuals and Groups

On any given day, student affairs practitioners, regardless of level of responsibility, may find themselves counseling individual students, advising student groups, teaching in the classroom, or giving a speech before a student assembly. All of these activities require the practitioner to understand how each student is unique, how students function as groups, and how students in the aggregate respond to and shape the campus environment. The knowledge base of the profession has given student affairs educators numerous theories to assist them in working with both individuals and groups of students.

Our work with individual students has been directed by a range of psychosocial, cognitive, and typology theories (Evans, Forney, and Guido-DiBrito, 1998). Through the work of Chickering and Reisser (1993), we have come to understand the developmental tasks in which our students are engaged. Theorists such as Josselson (1987), Cross (1971), Helms (1993), and D'Augelli (1994) help practitioners understand how gender, race, and sexual orientation shape identity. The cognitive processes students use to make sense of the world are explored by Baxter Magolda (1992), King and Kitchener (1994), and Perry (1968). Finally, a number of theorists (for example, Myers, 1980) posit that personality type plays an important role in human development. (Chapter Four examines many of these theories in greater detail and explores how these theoretical perspectives may need to be revised to consider the unique characteristics of Millennial students.)

These theories all focus on different aspects of development but share a common emphasis on the individual. Other theorists have offered us group perspectives for understanding students. Theories and models for understanding groups of students can be categorized under the headings of student peer group typologies, human aggregate perspectives, and cohort models.

Sanford's seminal *The American College* (1962) contains a chapter by Newcomb outlining the importance of student peer group influence. That work was extended by Clark and Trow (1966) through their development of a peer group typology that included student subcultures: academic, vocational, nonconformist, and collegiate. Using historical analysis, Horowitz (1987) finds similar student groups: college men and women, outsiders, and rebels. More recently, Kuh, Hu, and Vesper (2000) use data from the College Student Experiences Questionnaire and factor analytic techniques to develop a typology based on the activities in which students participate. They categorize students in these groups: disengaged, recreator, socializer, collegiate (similar to Clark and Trow's collegiate and Horowitz's college men and women), scientist, individualist, artist, grind, intellectual, and conventional. Readers are encouraged to examine the Kuh, Hu, and Vesper article as it features an excellent chart outlining a number of peer group typology models.

In addition to peer group typologies, a number of theories and models have been developed that more appropriately can be classified as human aggregate models (Strange and Banning, 2001). In addition to describing individuals, the Myers-Briggs model (Myers, 1980) can be used to explore how groups can be established on the basis of how the individuals in those groups gather information, make decisions about that information, and interact with the external world. John Holland's model (1973) of vocational choice can be used to describe individuals and also provides us with such useful aggregate concepts as congruence, consistency, and differentiation. At the heart of the human aggregate perspective is the idea that students are attracted to, stable in, and more satisfied with environments where other members of the environment share their personality characteristics or vocational preferences. This "birds of a feather flock together" approach has been used by student affairs and academic educators to direct a range of educational practices, from roommate matching (Rogers, 1990) to academic advising (Creamer and Scott, 2000).

The final group perspective is the cohort approach to understanding students. The Cooperative Institutional Research Program has been tracking the attitudes, beliefs, and behaviors of first-year students since 1966. By presenting normative data on entering college students since that time, researchers are able to discern changes in patterns of belief and behavior across time. Adelman (1994) engaged in similar longitudinal analysis using the National Longitudinal Study of the High School Class of 1972 to draw *Lessons of a Generation*. Levine (1981) and Levine and Cureton (1998) used cross-sectional data to paint portraits of college students in the late 1970s and 1990s. Levine and Cureton note that, "There is a preoccupation in this country with searching out the distinctive characteristics in every new generation of young people, the ways in which the current generation seems different from the last. We then apply an appropriate sobriquet that somehow captures the salient features of the age" (1998, p. 2).

Capturing the distinctive characteristics of a generation has been used by Jones (1980) to examine the impact of the Baby Boom generation on national politics, the economy, and culture. It has also been employed by Hirsh (1998) to explain the experiences of suburban youth in the mid-1990s and by Kitwana (2002) to examine the crisis facing young blacks in America.

The most extensive articulation of a generational model is that of William Strauss and Neil Howe. Their model has been the basis for examinations of generations of college students (Komives, 1993; Howe and Strauss, 2003) and forms the conceptual framework for much of this sourcebook. As such, the Strauss and Howe model warrants further discussion.

A Framework for Understanding Generations

By studying what Strauss and Howe (1991) describe as the "peer personality" of an emerging generation such as the Millennials (students born after 1980), student affairs practitioners can better identify their students' needs and reconcile the potential intergenerational conflicts that can emerge when values are not aligned. The relationships between Boomer generation or Generation X faculty and staff and the Millennial students now beginning to attend higher education can be better understood within the framework of generational analysis.

According to Strauss and Howe, each generation has its own biography, a biography that tells the story of how the personality of the generation is shaped and how that personality subsequently shapes other generations. In their model, generations are defined as "a cohort-group whose length approximates the span of a phase of life and whose boundaries are fixed by peer personality" (p. 60). By length, they assert that a "phase of life" involves central social roles that span a twenty-two-year period of an individual's life. Strauss and Howe build what they admit is a "simple lifecycle framework of four life phases of equal twenty-two-year lengths. Accordingly, we define 'youth' as lasting from ages 0 to 21; 'rising adulthood' from ages 22 to 43; 'midlife' from ages 44 to 65; and 'elderhood' from ages 66 to 87" (p. 56). Echoing the work of such life-span developmentalists as Erikson (1964), Levinson and Associates (1978), and Chickering and Havighurst (1981), Strauss and Howe suggest that the life roles at each life stage are distinctly different. For youth, the central role is one of dependence and includes growing, learning, accepting protection and nurturance, avoiding harm, and acquiring values. For the rising, activities include working, starting families and livelihoods, serving institutions, and testing values. For those in the midlife stage, leadership, parenting, teaching, directing institutions, and using values become important life tasks. Finally, elderhood entails stewardship, including supervising, mentoring, channeling endowments, and passing on values.

A generation also has a peer personality, which Strauss and Howe (1991) define as a "generational persona recognized and determined by (1) common age location; (2) common beliefs and behavior; and (3) perceived membership in a common generation" (p. 64). Each of these is important, but it may be the third one that is most important. To be a generation, its members must recognize it as distinct from other generations. What leads to this recognition is the interaction the members of a new generation have with members of other generations and how they experience "social moments," which Strauss and Howe define as "an era, typically lasting about a decade, when people perceive that historic events are radically altering their social environment" (p. 71).

This two-part interplay of one generation with another and with important social moments results in what Strauss and Howe term the "generational diagonal." The generational diagonal acknowledges that generations are not static; they move through time influencing and being influenced by important historical events (events Strauss and Howe see as inner-oriented "spiritual awakenings" and out-oriented "secular crises") and other generations.

The most interesting part of this theory is the idea that a generation is shaped by its interactions with other extant generations. In their newest book on Millennial students, Howe and Strauss (2003) posit a number of rules for understanding how generations move through the generational diagonal and interact with other generations:

First, each rising generation breaks with the young-adult generation, whose style no longer functions well in a new era.

Second, it corrects for what it perceives as the excesses of the current midlife generation—their parents and leaders—sometimes as a protest. . . .

Third, it fills the social role being vacated by the departing elder generation (p. 21).

As one views the current generations on college campuses, the dynamics of the interactions among these generations appear to give some credibility to these rules. Relative to the first rule, many members of the Millennial generation see themselves as a counterpoint to the generation that immediately preceded it (Generation X, or "Thirteeners") and not an extension of it. For instance, Millennial students prefer to work in teams rather than function as free agents, as do members of Generation X. The Millennials seem to have traded the apathy and aloofness of the Xers for a desire to become involved and tend to value authority rather than to be alienated from it (Lancaster and Stillman, 2002).

At the same time, Millennials are also attempting to correct some of the excesses of Baby Boom parents and grandparents. The narcissism and iconoclasm that marked the college years of the Boomers are in the process of being replaced by the conventionality and expectation of structure on the part of members of the Millennial generation (Howe and Strauss, 2000).

Most importantly to Strauss and Howe's theory of "generational cycles" (1991) is the relationship between the emerging Millennial students and the elderly GI generation. Howe and Strauss (2003) contend that "the most important link this 'G.I. Generation' has to today's teens is the void they leave behind: No other adult peer group possesses anything close to their upbeat, high-achieving, team-playing, and civic-minded reputation" (p. 22). Perhaps because of this perceived void, adults are encouraging Millennials to adopt the values of the GI generation. For their part, Millennials, in surveys, have responded that they have the highest regard for members of the GI generation and the lowest for members of Generation X (Howe and Strauss, 2000).

To fully understand this model, it is necessary to grasp the idea of dominant and recessive generations. Strauss and Howe indicate that certain generations become "dominant" because their members need to respond to crises as they move into rising adulthood and elderhood, whereas others are recessive because of the absence of such social moments. For instance, the dominance of the GI was the result of responding to both the Great Depression and World War II. The subsequent generation, whom Strauss and Howe label "Silents," are a recessive generation as a result of coming of age during a period of postwar peace and prosperity.

The final part of the Howe and Strauss generational theory is the manner in which the dynamics of diagonal movement result in a cycle of generational types that are recurrent in nature. In this regard, a dominant idealist generation, such as the Baby Boom generation, "grows up as increasingly indulged youths after a secular crisis" (Strauss and Howe, 1991, p. 74), as was faced by their parents, who were members of the GI generation. They are followed by a Reactive generation (Generation X) that "grows up as underprotected and criticized youths during a spiritual awakening, matures into risk-taking, alienated youths, mellows into pragmatic midlife leaders during a secular crisis and maintains respect (but less influence) as reclusive elders" (Strauss and Howe, 1991, p. 74). In the Strauss and Howe theory, this recessive generation would be followed by a dominant Civic generation, like the current Millennial generation. Members of such a generation "grow up as increasingly protected youth [who] will come of age during a secular crisis [for example, the War on Terrorism], will unite into a heroic and achieving cadre of rising adults, will build institutions as powerful midlifers and emerge as busy elders attacked by the next spiritual awakening" (Strauss and Howe, 1991, p. 74). Finally, there is a generation Howe and Strauss refer to as "Adaptive." Their example is the Silent generation, which they describe as recessive in nature. The Silents grew up as "overprotected and suffocated youth during a secular crisis, matured into risk-averse, conformist adults, and provided indecisive midlife leaders during a spiritual awakening before moving to less respected, but sensitive elderhood" (Strauss and Howe, 1991, p. 74).

These peer personalities move along a diagonal line of life stages that are buffeted by the influences of other generation peer personalities and social moments. What is important for this sourcebook is the proposition that, if knowledge of the values and motivations of student service providers as well as those to be served is understood, some guidance can be extended to make the provision of and reaction to these services most effective.

Current Generations on Campus

Four generations currently predominate on the nation's college campuses. In order, from the oldest to the youngest, they are Silents, Boomers, Thirteeners, and Millennials. This section presents a brief introduction to the demographics of each group as a way of setting the stage for the subsequent chapters in this sourcebook.

Silents (Birth Years 1925 to 1942). A recessive generation, Silents represent a rapidly declining proportion of the student, faculty, and administrative populations. Cutting-edge Silents are in their midseventies, while those born at the tail end of the generation are nearing retirement age. Strauss and Howe (1991) designate members of this generation "Silent" to recognize their position between two dominant generations: the GI generation of the Depression, World War II, and the postwar recovery; and the Baby Boomers of campus unrest, the Age of Aquarius, and the introspective

1970s and 1980s. Members of the Silent generation, who attended college as traditional-aged students, would have started their collegiate careers between 1943 and 1960. They attended college during a period Horowitz (1987) describes as one when "wealth and conservatism returned to campus. Upon the nation settled a sober mood that some students interpreted as a license to return the campus to college life" (p. 168).

Silents would have assumed positions as college faculty and administrators during the 1950s and 1960s and would have advanced in their professions during the 1970s, 1980s, and 1990s. According to the National Center for Education Statistics, in 1998 (the most current data available) members of the Silent generation constituted 25.8 percent of the full-time and part-time faculty in the nation's colleges and universities (National Center for Education Statistics, 2002). No similar data are available for staff and administrators on campus, but one is safe in assuming that a similar proportion of Silents would be found in those positions. Furthermore, in the five years since those data were collected, the number of Silents on campus has undoubtedly decreased, so the 25.8 percent certainly overrepresents members of that population. Silents are now turning over the reins of collegiate leadership to subsequent generations.

Boomers (Birth Years 1943 to 1960). This generation, described as a "very large mouse in a very small snake" (Hodgkinson, 1985, p. 1), has reached middle age and assumed the mantle of leadership from its Silent predecessors. Traditional-aged Boomers would have attended college between 1961 and 1982. Their college careers coincided with the civil rights and women's movements, the Vietnam War, and a period of significant collegiate unrest. Many of these students attended college during a period when "the social order seemed to be disintegrating" (Horowitz, 1987, p. 221). Many also extended their collegiate and postcollege educational careers into the 1980s and 1990; it was members of this group, as returning adult learners, who were responsible for significant enrollment growth on many college campuses in those decades.

In 1998, 50.6 percent of full-time and part-time faculty members were Boomers (National Center for Education Statistics, 2002). Once again, it is safe to assume that a similar proportion applies to administrators and staff members within college settings.

Thirteeners (Birth Years 1961 to 1981). Popularly referred to as Generation X (Strauss and Howe prefer the term *Thirteeners* to mark its place as the thirteenth generation since the Puritan generation that founded the nation), cutting-edge Thirteeners are now entering middle adulthood, while those at the tail end of the generation are wrapping up their college years and tackling the early adult tasks of partnering, developing a career and lifestyle structure, and assuming civic responsibility (Chickering and Havighurst, 1981).

A significant number of Thirteeners still remain in college; in 2002, more than 5.8 million Thirteeners were enrolled. That number represents, at a minimum, 37 percent of all the students enrolled in 2002 (National Center for Education Statistics, 2002). (Establishing the actual number of Thirteeners enrolled in 2002 is a difficult task. The upper age group divisions used by the NCES to report college enrollment breaks at thirty-five and includes all members born in 1967 or before. Therefore, this final NCES age grouping contains a significant number of Thirteeners as well as members of other generations.)

As already noted, Thirteeners are actively involved in the life task of building a career. Members of this generation account for 18 percent of all full-time and part-time faculty employed in 1998 (National Center for Education Statistics, 2002). It is conventional wisdom that the student affairs profession is a "young person's" profession. With that contention in mind, it is safe to assume that a significant number of student affairs administrators are members of this generation. The number of Thirteeners will only continue to increase in the years ahead, as the generation moves through the employment pipeline.

Millennials (Birth Years 1982 to 2002). Like their GI generation grandparents, members of the Millennial generation may have what Franklin D. Roosevelt called a "rendezvous with destiny." The assumption that generational greatness is potentially on the horizon is one of the reasons why there is so much attention being paid to Millennial students (Howe and Strauss, 2000; Martin and Tulgan, 2001; Sax, 2003). This generation will be the largest cohort in the nation's history, with census figures indicating some eighty million Americans born after 1981 (Yax, 2004). With an anticipated influx of immigrants potentially raising the number to more than ninety million, the Millennial generation would be 33 percent larger than the Baby Boom generation. It will also be the most diverse college-going generation ever. African American enrollment has more than doubled since 1980, and Hispanic enrollment is the fasting growing group (National Center for Education Statistics, 2002). Millennials are certainly the most educationally ambitious generation ever, with more than three out of four college freshmen projecting they will earn a graduate degree (Sax, 2003).

As the largest generation in our nation's history, the Millennial generation holds important implications for how colleges develop programs and policies during the initial decades of the twenty-first century. In 2002, approximately 6.9 million Millennials were enrolled in the nation's colleges and university, representing 44.2 percent of all students. By 2012, the number of Millennials is estimated to increase to 13.3 million, or 75 percent of all students. The number of Millennial students enrolled in 2012 will have increased by 93.5 percent over the 2002 level, while the number of students from other generations will decrease by 50.2 percent during that same ten-year period (National Center for Education Statistics, 2002).

In addition to changes in student demographics, cutting-edge Millennials will have established themselves in entry-level administrative and faculty positions by 2012. The first college graduates of the generation completed college in 2003. Those same students are now enrolling in student affairs preparation programs and are beginning to enter the administrative ranks in entry-level positions. Millennial generation faculty members should begin showing up on campuses by the end of this decade.

These demographics projections suggest the importance of understanding how this generation's values, beliefs, and behaviors are shaped and how to best educate and work with members of the Millennial generation. Subsequent chapters in this sourcebook lay out more detailed information on understanding, educating, and working with Millennials.

Conclusions and Caveats

A generational perspective provides student affairs educators with one more tool for understanding students. By exploring the factors that shape a generation's peer personality and discerning identifying characteristics of that personality, educators can develop more effective policies and practices. Effective practitioners must have a firm grasp of theoretical and conceptual models that explain their work. Student affairs has developed multiple theories for understanding students as individuals and as members of groups. Understanding the theory of generations gives the practitioner a supplemental source of insight to round out conceptual frameworks he or she already holds and relies on.

However, like all models, a generational perspective should be employed with caution. Like many megatheories, it can lead to stereotyping and overgeneralization. Still, it has been advanced by human resource development experts that people tend to do in the future what has worked for them in the past (Drucker, 1974). As long as this perspective is attached to consideration of the past behavior of an individual in order to predict the future, the theory has validity (Erikson, 1964). However, to make assumptions about another individual's behavior on the basis of knowledge of the previous individual's behavior would be erroneous. The same can be said of generations. One should not assume that a current generation's values, attitudes, and behaviors are the same as those of its immediate predecessors. A fascinating aspect of generational analysis is to observe the emerging generation's movement away from the previous generation's thematic values (Howe and Strauss, 2000). One should not study generations in order to predict the transferal of normative behaviors from one generation to the next. Rather, once a generation's themes are established, predictions about what motivates action through appealing to the goals, engendering the hopes, and appreciating the fears of a particular generation can emerge.

Like measures of central tendency, a generational approach may illuminate the characteristics of the group, but it also obscures the idiographic characteristics of the individual. The information contained in this and subsequent chapters should prove useful in understanding the Millennial generation, but it may prove woefully inadequate for understanding any specific

Millennial student. Furthermore, one must always approach with caution the use of such models for understanding the dynamics of subcultures on college campuses. Strauss and Howe developed their theory by examining the big picture of historical and cultural events that shape generations. However, the big picture seldom contains images of marginalized groups. It is uncertain how effectively the generational perspective can be applied to students of color, LGBT students, and students of specific ethnic and cultural groups. These students must interact with larger cultural forces and are members of their generational cohort, so one would assume they share many of the same experiences and perspectives. However, the lesson learned from other social science perspectives—that the variance within groups is always greater than the variance between groups—undoubtedly applies to generations as well.

References

Adelman, C. *Lessons of a Generation.* San Francisco: Jossey-Bass, 1994.

Astin, A. W. *What Matters in College? Four Critical Years Revisited.* San Francisco: Jossey-Bass, 1995.

Baxter Magolda, M. B. *Knowing and Reasoning in College: Gender-Related Patterns in Students' Intellectual Development.* San Francisco: Jossey-Bass, 1992.

Chickering, A. W., and Havighurst, R. J. "The Life Cycle." In A. W. Chickering and Associates, *The Modern American College.* San Francisco: Jossey-Bass, 1981.

Chickering, A. W., and Reisser, L. *Education and Identity* (2nd ed.). San Francisco: Jossey-Bass, 1993.

Clark, R., and Trow, M. "The Organizational Context." In T. M. Newcomb and E. K. Wilson (eds.), *College Peer Groups: Problems and Prospects for Research.* Hawthorne, N.Y.: Aldine de Gruyter, 1966.

Creamer, C. A., and Scott, D. W. "Assessing Individual Advisor Effectiveness." In V. N. Gordon and W. R. Habley (eds.), *Academic Advising: A Comprehensive Handbook.* San Francisco: Jossey-Bass, 2000.

Cross, W. E., Jr. "Toward a Psychology of Black Liberation: The Negro-to-Black Conversion Experience." *Black World,* 1971, *20*(9), 13–27.

D'Augelli, A. R. "Identity Development and Sexual Orientation: Toward a Model of Lesbian, Gay, and Bisexual Development." In E. J. Trickett, R. J. Watts, and D. Birman (eds.), *Human Diversity: Perspectives on People in Context.* San Francisco: Jossey-Bass, 1994.

Drucker, P. F. *Management: Tasks, Responsibilities, and Practices.* New York: HarperCollins, 1974.

Erikson, E. H. *Insight and Responsibility.* New York: Norton, 1964.

Evans, N. J., Forney, D. S., and Guido-DiBrito, F. *Student Development in College: Theory, Research, and Practice.* San Francisco: Jossey-Bass, 1998.

Helms, J. E. *Black and White Racial Identity: Theory, Research and Practice.* New York: Praeger, 1993.

Hirsh, P. *A Tribe Apart: A Journey into the Heart of American Adolescence.* New York: Ballantine Books, 1998.

Hodgkinson, H. L. *All One System: Demographics of Education, Kindergarten Through Graduate School.* Washington, D.C.: Institute for Educational Leadership, 1985.

Holland, J. L. *Making Vocational Choices: A Theory of Careers.* Upper Saddle River, N.J.: Prentice Hall, 1973.

Horowitz, H. L. *Campus Life: Undergraduate Cultures from the End of the Eighteenth Century to the Present.* New York: Knopf, 1987.

Howe, N., and Strauss, W. *Millennials Rising: The Next Great Generation.* New York: Vintage Books, 2000.

Howe, N., and Strauss, W. *Millennials Go to College.* Great Falls, Va.: American Association of Registrars and Admissions Officers and LifeCourse Associates, 2003.

Jones, L. Y. *Great Expectations: America and the Baby Boom Generation.* New York: Ballantine Books, 1980.

Josselson, R. *Finding Herself: Pathways to Identity Development in Women.* San Francisco: Jossey-Bass, 1987.

King, P. M., and Kitchener, K. S. *Developing Reflective Judgment: Understanding and Promoting Intellectual Growth and Critical Thinking in Adolescents and Adults.* San Francisco: Jossey-Bass, 1994.

Kitwana, B. *The Hip Hop Generation: Young Blacks and the Crisis in African-American Culture.* New York: BasicCivitas Books, 2002.

Komives, S. R. "Back to the Future: Class of 1996." *NASPA Journal,* 1993, *31*(1), 64–71.

Kuh, G. D., Hu, S., and Vesper, N. "They Shall Be Known by What They Do: An Activities-Based Typology of College Students." *Journal of College Student Development,* 2000, *41*(2), 228–244.

Lancaster, L. C., and Stillman, D. *When Generations Collide.* New York: HarperBusiness, 2002.

Levine, A. *When Dreams and Heroes Died: A Portrait of Today's College Student.* San Francisco: Jossey-Bass, 1981.

Levine, A., and Cureton, J. S. *When Hope and Fear Collide: A Portrait of Today's College Student.* San Francisco: Jossey-Bass, 1998.

Levinson, D. J., and Associates. *The Seasons of a Man's Life.* New York: Knopf, 1978.

Martin, C. A., and Tulgan, B. *Managing Generation Y.* New Haven, Conn.: HRD Press, 2001.

Myers, I. B. *Gifts Differing.* Palo Alto, Calif.: Consulting Psychologists Press, 1980.

National Center for Education Statistics. *Digest of Education Statistics, 2002.* Washington, D.C.: National Center for Education Statistics, 2002. Retrieved October 12, 2003 from http://nces.ed.gov/pubs2003/digest02/index.asp.

Newcomb, T. M. "Student Peer-Group Influence." In N. Sanford (ed.), *The American College: A Psychological and Social Interpretation of Higher Learning.* New York: Wiley, 1962.

Pascarella, E. T., and Terenzini, P. T. *How College Affects Students.* San Francisco: Jossey-Bass, 1991.

Perry, W. *Forms of Intellectual and Ethical Development in the College Years: A Scheme.* Austin, Tex.: Holt, Rinehart, and Winston, 1968.

Rogers, R. B. "An Integration of Campus Ecology and Student Development: The Olentangy Project." In D. G. Creamer and Associates, *College Student Development: Theory and Practice for the 1990s.* Alexandria, Va.: American College Personnel Association, 1990.

Sanford, N. (ed.). *The American College: A Psychological and Social Interpretation of Higher Learning.* New York: Wiley, 1962.

Sax, L. J. "Our Incoming Students: What Are They Like?" *About Campus,* 2003, *8*(3), 15–20.

Strange, C. C., and Banning, J. H. *Educating by Design: Creating Campus Learning Environments That Work.* San Francisco: Jossey-Bass, 2001.

Strauss, W., and Howe, N. *Generations: The History of America's Future, 1584 to 2069.* New York: Morrow, 1991.

Yax, L. K. *Projected Population of the United States, by Age and Sex: 2000 to 2050.* Washington, D.C.: U.S. Bureau of the Census, 2004. Retrieved Apr. 27, 2004, from http://www.census.gov/ipc/www/usinterimproj.

MICHAEL D. COOMES is associate professor of higher education and student affairs at Bowling Green State University in Ohio.

ROBERT DEBARD is associate professor of higher education and student affairs and interim director of the School of Leadership and Policy Studies at Bowling Green State University in Ohio.

2

Generations are shaped by history and embedded in culture. This chapter explores how history and popular culture can be useful lenses for understanding generations.

Understanding the Historical and Cultural Influences That Shape Generations

Michael D. Coomes

In the summer of 1989, recent high school graduates ready to enter college might have watched the Chinese government suppress the democratic student movement by massacring its adherents in Tiananmen Square. Until that time, the dominant historical events that shaped the worldview of these soon-to-be first-year students were likely the explosion of the *Challenger* space shuttle; the Iran hostage crisis; and a number of ecological disasters, including Bhopal (1984), Chernobyl (1986), and the wreck of the *Exxon Valdez* (1989). Other larger societal events that certainly affected the lives of these eighteen-year-olds would have included the stock market crash of 1987 and the subsequent economic downturn; an increase in youth crime; declining test scores; and the continuing disintegration of cultural institutions such as the church, schools, and the family.

These eighteen-year-olds would have grown up on "Sesame Street" and eventually moved to MTV (which premiered in 1981). They traveled to a galaxy far, far, away as six-year-olds and rode bikes with *ET* at eleven. By 1989, rap music was ten years old and "Fight the Power" by Public Enemy was one of the year's top songs. On television that year, they saw contrasting pictures of American family life portrayed by the "Cosby Show" and "Roseanne" and could follow a significant portion of the American life span by watching the "Wonder Years" and the "Golden Girls." Finally, lucky graduates may have been the first on their block to own the new handheld video game called the Gameboy.

Contrast the entering first-year students of 1989 with the first-year students of 2003. The latter (members of the Millennial generation, as opposed to the preceding students from Generation X) were born in 1985. They would have little direct memory of the fall of communism, the first Gulf War, or the Los Angeles riots of 1992. The dominant historical events shaping their worldview were the O. J. Simpson trial, the bombing of the Murrah Federal Building in Oklahoma City, Princess Diana's death, the Columbine High School shootings, and the terrorist attacks of September 11, 2001. Their space shuttle disaster involved the *Columbia,* not the *Challenger.* They were children and adolescents during a period of economic growth. During their lifetime, they only knew four presidents—Ronald Reagan, George H. W. Bush, Bill Clinton, and George W. Bush—but probably had functional memories of only the latter two. As a group, they came from families who focused on their children, experienced the continuing diversification of the nation's population, and grew up during a time of declining crime (including, contrary to public opinion, school crime; Brooks, Schiraldi, and Ziedenberg, 2000).

Like the members of their predecessor generation, they too grew up on "Sesame Street," but they also toured the world with Carmen Sandiego. They attended grade school with the Olsen Twins and entered adolescence with Harry Potter. They learned the number one hits from "Total Request Live," their sense of geography from "Road Rules," and how to live in a group from "Real World." Their image of family life came from the Simpsons (and later, perhaps, the Osbornes). They grew up on boy bands like NSYNC and the Backstreet Boys; the grrrl-powered music of Britney Spears, Alanis Morissette, and the Spice Girls; and the rap of Eminem, Lauryn Hill, and 50 Cent. They played with Cabbage Patch Kids and Teenaged Mutant Ninja Turtles, watched the *Titanic* sink, and entered the *Matrix.* They moved from CDs to MP3s and are the first generation to hook up through cell phones and instant messaging (IM).

As these vignettes demonstrate, two powerful forces—history and popular culture—play an important role in shaping the values, beliefs, attitudes, and worldviews of individuals and groups. History and popular culture are inextricably intertwined (Nachbar and Lause, 1992). History is, the dictionary tells us, a "chronological record of significant events usually including an explanation of their causes." Culture is defined as "the customary beliefs, social forms and material traits of. . . . social groups." By these definitions, history is a process and culture a product. This chapter presents a brief primer on the uses of history and popular culture as guides for understanding generations. In addition to exploring the uses of history and pop culture for understanding generations, this chapter also presents an overview of historical events and popular culture trends that have shaped the development of Millennial students.

History as a Guide for Understanding Generations

It is quite clear that the major political and economic events of the Great Depression of the 1930s and the Second World War played an important formative role in shaping the "greatest generation" (Brokaw, 1998). Following their defeat of fascism, this GI generation returned home to enter college in record numbers, was responsible for rebuilding the economies and infrastructures of their defeated enemies, "helped convert a wartime economy into the most powerful peacetime economy in history" (Brokaw, 1998, p. xx), and made important contributions to science, technology, and the arts. Brokaw certainly shares Strauss and Howe's sentiment (1991) that, "just as history produces generations, so too do generations produce history" (p. 35).

Numerous historians have explored the relationship of generations to the shape of history. The great Spanish philosopher José Ortega y Gasset explores the concept in a number of his writings, notably *The Revolt of the Masses* (1932), *Mission of the University* (1942/1992), and *Man and Crisis* (1933; Graham, 1997). Ortega y Gasset's ideas of the duration and cyclical nature of generations have influenced other social scientists and historians, among them Marías (1967) and Schlesinger (1986). Since Schlesinger's cyclical model deals explicitly with American history, it is the most appropriate for this discussion and should be explicated in greater detail.

Schlesinger (1986) draws upon the works of a number of historians and essayists (including his own father, Arthur Schlesinger, Sr.; Ralph Waldo Emerson; and Henry Adams) to make the case for the cyclical nature of history. Borrowing from others, he suggests that the ebb and flow of history swings between periods of innovation and conservatism, a concern with the rights of the few and the wrongs of the many, and an emphasis on public purpose and private interest. Levine (1981) also discerns this tension of a historical period emphasizing public purpose being followed by one stressing private interest.

Using analysis of the values and beliefs of college students in the 1970s as well as insights drawn from sociology and psychology, Levine proposes that society oscillates between periods of community ascendancy and periods of individual ascendancy. The former is characterized by a sense of duty to others, a "concern for responsibility, acceptance of the propriety of giving, future orientation, focus on the commonalities people share, [and an] ascetic" outlook (Levine, 1981, p. 25). These community-oriented periods are followed by periods of individual ascendancy, which are typified by a focus on the self, a "concern with rights, acceptance of the propriety of taking, present orientation, a focus on differences among people, [and a] hedonistic" outlook (Levine, 1981, p. 25). It is the interplay of these alternating periods of public purpose or community ascendancy and private interest or individual ascendancy that shapes the lives and character of a generation. As Schlesinger notes: "Each new phase must flow out of the conditions—and contradictions—of the phase before and then itself prepare the way for the next recurrence. A true cycle, in other words, is self-generating. It cannot be determined, short of catastrophe, by external events" (p. 27).

But, Schlesinger points out, the patience and stamina of the American public for actively engaging in civic life or for remaining quiescent and inner-focused are limited. The outward focus on public purpose is demanding, challenging, and ultimately draining. Periods of public action tend to foster large-scale change in a short period of time (Schlesinger, 1986). The civil rights, women's, and antiwar movements of the 1960s resulted in numerous social and political changes. For example, in 1964–65 Congress enacted some the most far-reaching social legislation since the New Deal of the Franklin Roosevelt Administration. Important domestic legislation enacted in that time period included the Civil Rights Act of 1964; the Economic Opportunity Act of 1964, which created the Job Corps and VISTA; the Elementary and Secondary Education Act of 1965; the Voting Rights Act of 1965; and the Higher Education Act of 1965, which formed the foundation for the nation's current federal student aid system (Coomes, 2004). It is understandable that a period of such radical social change, typified by civil disobedience, demands for social justice, demonstrations, and riots, would eventually lead to exhaustion. That exhaustion in the cause of public action led to an inevitable period of introspection and focus on the individual. The 1960s were followed by the 1970s, a period labeled the "Me Decade" by Tom Wolfe (1976/1987) and typified by a "tide of narcissism" (Abrams, n.d.). The decade of the 1970s included important historical events, such as the end of the Vietnam War, Watergate, and the resignation of President Nixon; but it also included, "among some portions of the population, a turning inward to the pleasures of self-improvement, a setting aside of traditional sexual mores and new emphasis on jogging, aerobics classes and even a massage technique called Rolfing" (Abrams, n.d., sect. 3).

Ortega y Gasset (1944/1992) establishes the length of time of a historical generation at approximately thirty years. During the first fifteen-year span, the generation seeks to establish its own ideals and direction by countering those established by its predecessor. During the second half of the thirty-year span, the generation comes to power and its ideas and ideals predominate until being set aside by the following generation (Schlesinger, 1986). This thirty-year cycle should not be construed as inviolate or repetitive. In addition to alternating between periods of public purpose and private interest, history does have a sense of forward motion. Moving from public purpose to private interest and back again does not result in a return to the status quo; "liberal reforms usually survived after conservatives regained power" (Schlesinger, 1986, p. 24). According to Schlesinger, the appropriate metaphor for the cyclical nature of history is the spiral "in which the alternation [proceeds] at successively higher levels and [allows] for the culmination of change" (p. 24).

History in the Lives of Millennials

Although the Millennial generation is just entering early adulthood, it is possible to discern a number of historical trends that will shape its future: new puritanism (Phillips, 1999), political polarization and ineffectiveness, millennial mania, and tension between globalization and nationalism as well as fundamentalism and postmodernity.

For much of the lives of the Millennial generation, the larger culture of the United States has struggled with balancing the need for openness and a desire to keep young people and the nation safe. This drive for safety has resulted in numerous initiatives that reflect a new Puritanism. Starting in the mid-1980s with voluntary agreements by the recording industry to place parental advisory stickers on music, efforts have been made to protect young people from sex and violence in a number of media. In 1996, Congress passed the Communications Decency Act to regulate inappropriate material on the Internet. That legislation was quickly declared unconstitutional, and parents turned to blocking software to regulate what their children could view on the Web (Tapscott, 1998). Similarly, legislation was passed in 1998 to require incorporation of the V-chip (which allows parents to block the television shows their children might watch) in all new televisions (Rutenberg, 2001). Other examples of the new Puritanism include bans on smoking, concerns about drug and alcohol abuse, and calls for safer sex practices. Much like Prohibition in the 1920s, bans against smoking have been instituted to ensure that Americans avoid temptation and health risks. Members of the Millennial generation were educated in DARE (Drug Abuse Resistance Education) programs and urged to say no to drugs and alcohol. Similar concerns about binge drinking on college campuses have resulted in new policies and research on the topic of collegiate alcohol abuse. Driven by concerns about sexually transmitted diseases, Millennial students are being encouraged to abstain from premarital sex completely or, if sexually active, practice "safer sex" (Mangan, 1995). Finally, a strain of the new Puritanism could be seen in the reaction of many in the United States to the sexual indiscretions that led to the impeachment of President William Jefferson Clinton (Phillips, 1999; "Impeachment and Beyond," 1998).

The Clinton impeachment and its aftermath demonstrate another set of trends shaping the worldviews of Millennials: political polarization and ineffectiveness (Pew Research Center, 2003). A review of data from the Cooperative Institutional Research Project from 1982 to 2002 shows that the political views of college freshmen are becoming more polarized at the expense of the middle. In 1982, 21.9 percent of college freshmen rated themselves as far left and liberal, 57 percent as middle of the road, and 21.1 percent as conservative and far right (Astin, Oseguera, Sax, and Korn, 2002). By 2002 those proportions were 27.8 percent far left and liberal, 50.8 percent middle of the road, and 21.3 percent conservative and far right (Sax and others, 2002). When surveyed about a range of social issues, Millennials in 2002 also demonstrated a bifurcation of opinion, as respondents were just as likely to support conservative positions as liberal ones. According to the 2002 Freshman Survey, the majority of respondents supported conservative positions on the rights of criminals, legalization of marijuana, and abolition of the death penalty. Concurrently, they held more liberal views on issues such as handgun control, curbs against racist and sexist speech, and marital rights for same-sex couples. Echoing larger societal trends, the first-year respondents were nearly equally split on the key issues of reproductive rights (53.6 percent agreed abortion should be legal), taxing the wealthy (50 percent agreed the wealthy should pay a larger share of taxes), and abolishing affirmative action in college admissions (49 percent agreed that it should be abolished; Sax and others, 2002).

Whether this political polarization is a cause or a result of the political ineffectiveness that has gripped the nation since conservative Republicans claimed control of the House of Representatives in 1994 is difficult to establish. However, most would agree that politics has become more coarse and divisive in the past fifteen years. Impeachments, contested elections, recalls, attack ads, and ineffectual leadership have led to public disillusionment with government, as demonstrated by the fact that slightly over half (51.3 percent) of the voting-age public voted in the 2000 presidential election (Federal Election Commission, n.d.). The discourse of American politics transpires at a scream. Pundits of the left (for example, Michael Moore) and the right (for example, Rush Limbaugh) find it easier to stake ideologically pure claims to truth than engage in the difficult task of collaboration and consensus. The Millennial generation is being lauded for its conciliatory nature. Whether it will use those skills of reconciliation to bridge the political divide or succumb to the politics of difference remains to be seen.

The turning of the millennium brought with it an increased interest in eschatology and spiritualism. In an interesting twist on the connection between the turning of a millennium and the end times, 1999 saw a significant portion of society consumed by "Y2K" fears of a technological meltdown. The turning of the millennium was also accompanied by renewed interest in all things spiritual. This is not surprising when one considers that the two dominant generations of the age, Boomers and Millennials, were involved at the turn of the century in life tasks that focused on the inward, spiritual dimensions of life. A 2003 survey conducted by the Higher Education Research Institute found that "more than two-thirds of third-year undergraduate students demonstrate a substantial level of religious engagement and commitment" as evidence by their engagement in prayer, attendance at religious services, and discussions of religion or spirituality with peers (Astin and others, 2003, p. 2).

Cimino and Lattin (1998), in exploring the dimensions of faith in the new century, see a number of patterns: the continuing separation of spirituality and formal religious institutions; a "pick and choose" approach to faith, which empowers seekers to borrow the most useful doctrines and practices from a range of faith traditions; a continuation of the movement of spirituality into other areas of life, including work and education; and the popularization of faith. The latter is particularly appropriate for this chapter and its focus on popular culture. As Cimino and Lattin (1998) state, "as entertainment media becomes the primary conveyor of common culture, it will compete with religious groups as the main bearer of spiritual and religious insight" (p. 38). The connection between faith and popular culture is also shared by Beaudoin (1998), who connects generational analysis, popular culture, and spirituality.

The final historical tides that are shaping the lives of the Millennial generation were building prior to September 11, 2001, but have become stronger since the events of that tragic day. Those tides include a tension between nationalism and globalization and the rift between fundamentalism and postmodernity (Friedman, 2002). Not since the 1930s has the United States struggled so fitfully with the competing desires to engage with the larger world or turn inward and limit its interaction with others. Those competing demands evince themselves in a number of ways: discussion of the responsibilities of the world's only superpower to fulfill peacekeeping and humanitarian efforts, engagement with the United Nations, immigration policy, trade, and battling the worldwide war on terrorism.

It is this last issue that has resulted in increased cognizance of the difference between the postmodern worldview of the United States and the fundamentalist worldview of many other nations. In discussing a nascent movement away from fundamentalism in Iran, Friedman notes: "Islamic reformation. . . . is still hugely important, because it reflects a deepening understanding by many Iranian Muslims that to thrive in the modern era they, and other Muslims, need an Islam different from the lifeless, antimodern, anti-Western fundamentalism being imposed in Iran and propagated by the Saudi Wahhabi clerics. This understanding is the necessary condition for preventing the brewing crisis between Islam and the West— which was triggered by 9/11—from turning into a war of civilizations" (2002, p. 31).

Creating a United States that can actively assist other nations in their own development while preserving the peace and protecting our security may be the most difficult task facing Millennials. For guidance, they may want to turn to the history of the last civic generation, the GIs, who successfully engaged with and helped rebuild the world following the Second World War.

The Pop Culture Lens

Just as historical events shape the values, beliefs, and attitudes of a generation, so do larger cultural trends. When considering culture and its influences, it is necessary to differentiate between three types of culture: elite, popular, and folk (Nachbar and Lause, 1992). Elite culture consists of those aspects of the culture that "are produced by and for a limited number of people who have specialized interests, training or knowledge" (1992, p. 15). Elite culture, or high culture (Gripsrud, 1998), requires one to be cognizant of not just the art or the creation but also the artist or creator. Elite culture requires one to be interested in and knowledgeable about it. One seldom comes to appreciate the ballet or opera without some understanding of its origins, artists, and history. Juxtaposed to elite culture is folk culture, which "refers to the products of human work and thought (culture) that have developed within a limited community and that are communicated directly from generation to generation, between 'folk' who are familiar to each other" (Nachbar and Lause, 1992, p. 15). Folk culture is typically transmitted orally; the origin of the artifact or event is generally unknown, and it is generally "simple both thematically and technologically" (p. 15). According to Nachbar and Lause, much of what counts as campus culture (see Bronner, 1990; and Steinberg, 1992) can be classified as folk culture. The final categorization, and the focus of this chapter, is popular culture, "the products of human work and thought which are (or have been) accepted and approved of by a large community or population" (Nachbar and Lause, 1992, p. 14). Using this definition, there are no assumptions about quality or timelessness. Furthermore, the definition accommodates the inclusion of cultural forms from subgroups (for example, youth culture or queer culture) in the larger mass culture.

Using concepts similar to those developed by Kuh and Whitt (1998) and Schein (1992), Nachbar and Lause (1992) have developed a model for explaining popular culture. Employing the metaphor of the house, they suggest that popular culture consists of (1) cultural mind-sets, (2) artifacts (objects and people), and (3) events that are encountered in daily life.

The cultural mind-set consists of bedrock beliefs (myths) and values, along with more clearly articulated beliefs and values. Ortega y Gasset (1941) suggests that "beliefs constitute the basic stratum, that which lies deepest, in the architecture of our life. By them we live, and by the same token we rarely think of them" (p. 174). These beliefs are generally tacitly held (Schein, 1992) and are not open to regular questioning and criticism. Layered on this bedrock are more visible beliefs and values. Nachbar and Lause distinguish them from the former in that they are shallow, transient, faddish, and prone to fancies and fashion.

Because beliefs and values (particularly the bedrock type) are difficult to discern, it is necessary to have physical representations to grasp and understand them. This is the level of the artifact—the people and objects that embody the values. Popular people are considered heroes or celebrities and popular objects are icons. These heroes/celebrities and icons can be imaginary (Superman, the sleigh "Rosebud" in the film *Citizen Kane*) or real (Samuel L. Jackson, the Liberty Bell). Celebrities cut across the real-imaginary boundary. They do exist as objective realities (Madonna exists) but "their hyped-up, fabricated star persona is often so distant from the real person as to be more properly considered a type of fiction" (Nachbar and Lause, 1992, p. 24). Similarly, Nachbar and Lause note that stereotypes cut across and contain elements of both the real and the imaginary. Where celebrities are typically positive, stereotypes are frequently negative, particularly when employed to label groups that do not subscribe to dominant culture values or that have been marginalized by the larger mass culture.

The final level, which shapes and is shaped by preceding levels, is the event. Nachbar and Lause include rituals, popular arts, and their connective tissue—formula—at this level: "Rituals are highly patterned events in which we all participate as a way of marking important passages in our individual lives or in society as a whole, in which we bind our culture together in a celebration of our common beliefs and values and/or in which we release tension and anxiety in a socially acceptable, 'safe' manner" (Nachbar and Lause, 1992, p. 27).

Manning (2000) and Magolda (2000, 2001) have pointed out the importance of rituals (such as move-in day or the campus tour) as means for building a sense of community on campus. The popular arts are so vast that many who study popular culture see them as popular culture (Nachbar and Lause, 1992). However, although "they are vast and diverse. . . . they do not stand isolated from the other [levels] and they derive their meaning from the beliefs and values. . . . of the popular mindset" (Nachbar and Lause, 1992, p. 28). Formulas are the patterns that identify a genre of art (the mystery novel, the science fiction story, the soap opera) as well as steps that give rituals "their order and identity" (Nachbar and Lause, 1992, p. 29).

The importance of popular culture should not be trivialized. The study of popular culture is important as a means for understanding the underlying values and beliefs that guide our culture, and because it is infinitely accessible it may be the best entry point for understanding those beliefs and values. Furthermore, as Giroux contends, popular culture has important educational implications:

> As I have argued elsewhere, learning in the postmodern age is located elsewhere—in popular spheres that shape their [youths'] identities through forms of knowledge and desire that appear absent from what is taught in school. The literacies of the postmodern age are electronic, aural, and image based; and it is precisely within the diverse terrain of popular culture that pedagogical practices must be established as part of a broader politics of public life—practices that will aggressively subject dominant power to criticism, analysis,

and transformation as part of a progressive reconstruction of democratic society [Giroux, 1998, p. 49].

In addition to having a structure, popular culture comes in numerous forms: print media, film, television, music, fashion, computer media, sport, and games. Each of these cultural forms is dense, vast, and highly complex; each can be a separate window on the culture or combined with other forms to develop a more complex picture of the popular culture. Consider, for example, film. At its most basic, one might divide it between documentary and fictional films. The latter can be divided further, for example, into dramas, comedies, musicals, horror films, science fiction, westerns, and war movies. Films that center on monsters, haunted houses, psychopaths, and ghosts all fall under the horror heading. Monster movies might employ BEMs (bugged-eyed monsters, as in *Alien*), vampires, werewolves, mummies, invisible men, zombies, and large beasts. Dividing the large-beast category allows us to consider how King Kong can morph into Godzilla, who becomes the Stay Puff Marshmallow Man of *Ghostbusters*. Each form can be similarly deconstructed, leading to a complex of perspectives and ideas.

As is the case with much in youth culture, it is necessary to move beyond the immediately evident forms and find alternative and fugitive sources of insight. Magazines such as *YM, Teen People,* or *Thrasher* help educators understand how the dominant culture of mass-market magazines interprets and shapes youth culture, but to understand how youth views itself and mass culture it may be more useful to read youth-generated "zines" like *Spank* (http://www.spankmag.com).

Readers familiar with postmodern critique, literary criticism, and new historicism will find the analytical lenses for examining popular culture quite familiar. According to Strinati (1995), scholars have used structuralism, semiology, Marxism, feminism, and postmodernism to examine, understand, and critique forms of popular culture. Readers seeking further insight into the use of various analytical perspectives for exploring popular culture are referred to Strinati (1995) and Storey (1998).

Pop Culture Trends in the Lives of Millennials

As noted by Giroux, popular culture has played an educative role in the lives of the Millennial generation. This section suggests some general pop culture trends that have influenced how Millennials see and interact with the world. Where appropriate, cultural forms are suggested to support the trend identified.

PC, PS2, DVD, CD, and MP3. As seen in Chapter Three, one of the defining characteristics of the Millennial generation is its technological literacy. They are truly the children of the computer age. Personal computers came of age in the early 1980s (the IBM PC was introduced in 1981, the Apple Macintosh in 1984) just as members of the Millennial generation were being born. They have grown up with the Internet, e-mail, and IM. Their computer skills have been refined by playing video games on a series of gaming platforms: the Nintendo Entertainment System, or NES (1985); Gameboy (1988); Super Nintendo (1991); Sony Playstation (1995); Nintendo 64 (1996); PS2 (2000); Gamecube (2001); and X-Box (2001). According to a 2002 survey by the Pew Project on the Internet and American Life (Jones, 2003), 70 percent of college students reported playing video, computer, or online games. Survey respondents reported that gaming had "mostly positive and few negative effects on their social lives" and little impact at all on academic performance (Jones, 2003, p. 9).

In addition to video and computer gaming, Millennials grew up watching videotapes, dabbled for a short period with laserdiscs, and moved to digital video discs (DVD). By 2003, fifty-four million DVD players had been sold (Digital Bits, 2003). Their music has almost always come on compact disc (CD) but is rapidly being replaced by digitized music available online (MP3). The ready availability of downloadable and swappable music has caused considerable concern among copyright holders (Gorey, 2003; Kiernan, 2002), forced universities to confront their role in music and software piracy (Carlson, 2003), and placed a strain on institutional computing resources (Carlson, 2001).

Grrrl Power. From an early age, young Millennial girls have seen images portraying strong, independent, and capable women. These images have resulted in acknowledgments of a trend to greater empowerment for young women from entities as diverse as the Girl Scouts of America ("Secretary Shalala Unveils. . . . ," 1998) and *Rolling Stone* magazine (Dunn, 1999).

Girls, for the first time in American history, wield tangible power in dictating popular culture, and they are confident consumers, secure in their opinions. A cottage industry has sprung up around the study of these young'uns, because what they dig will eventually make its way, in diluted form, to the forty-year-olds (Dunn, 1999, p. 120).

Here are examples, drawn from a variety of pop culture forms, that demonstrate the emergence of Grrrl Power. In animated film, *The Little Mermaid* (1989); *Beauty and the Beast* (1991); *Pocahontas* (1995); *Anastasia* (1998); *Mulan* (1998); *Spirited Away* (2002). In sport, the WNBA; USA 1999 Women's World Cup Champions; the Williams sisters, Mia Hamm, Sarah Hughes, Tara Dakides. In magazines, *Cosmo Girl, Seventeen, Teen People, YM*. In music, Beyonce Knowles, Avril Lavigne, Alanis Morissette, Britney Spears, the Spice Girls. On television, the Olsen Twins, "Buffy the Vampire Slayer," "Clarissa Explains It All," "The Gilmore Girls."

Hip Hop Goes Mainstream. Its prevalence and emergence with the Millennial generation make the case for considering rap music (or just rap) the soundtrack of the generation. Boomers had psychedelic rock, Thirteeners had grunge, and Millennials have rap. Rap can trace its roots to African and Afro-American oral traditions, R & B, disco, and reggae (Njubi, 2001). Rap comes in multiple styles: gangsta, message, and pop (Njubi, 2001); East Coast and West Coast; and even Christian rap. Rap is performed by men (Nelly) and women (Lil' Kim) and by individual artists (Eminem) and groups (Black Eyed Peas). Hip hop, the culture that has grown up around rap, has had a significant impact on the larger mass culture. Kitwana (2002) makes the claim that "within the arena of popular culture, rap music more than anything else has helped shape the new Black youth culture" (p. 9). It has also helped shape the larger culture. The influence of rap and hip hop can be see in television commercials, fashion (FUBU, "old style" athletic jerseys), and film ("hood" films such as *Menace to Society* and *Set It Off*; Kitwana, 2002).

Hip hop's emergence as an important cultural force has not come without criticism. Like comic books (Wright, 2001) and rock and roll before it, rap (especially gangsta rap) has been criticized for supporting messages that conflict with dominant culture values—particularly around the issues of sex, violence, and misogynism (Lipsitz, 1998). Criticism aside, rap and hip hop culture have played and will continue to play an important role in defining the values and perspectives of members of the Millennial generation.

Reach out and Touch Someone—Constantly. Millennials have mastered the art of attachment. They have found a multitude of ways for staying connected, including talking or texting on cell phones, instant messaging their friends, staying connected to distant parents through e-mail, reading and posting to public bulletin boards, and just entering their philosophical ramblings in their personal blog (short for Web log; Foroohar and Itoi, 2003).

Cell phones are ubiquitous on campus. Millennials are driving the cell phone market, attracted by the opportunity to customize their cell phones with designer wraps and unique ring tones and use them for text messaging, photography, and game play (Mack, 2003; Morris, 2003). The use of cell phones and text messaging has even presented challenges for teaching as the ringing of cell phones disrupts classes and students find new ways to use them to share information during tests (Young, 2003).

Staying connected 24–7, Millennials are redefining the meaning of interpersonal maturity. E-mail, cell phones, and IM allow Millennials to cast a much wider net of relationships. Those technologies also allow Millennials the opportunity to avoid the difficult task of confronting others face-to-face. It is much easier to ditch a class electronically than call and speak with the professor; it is certainly more comfortable to terminate a relationship through e-mail or IM-ing than by sitting down and talking with the other person. At the same time, the anonymity offered by e-mail, IM, and classroom electronic discussion boards may make it easier for introverts to participate in discourse. These new communication methods and their appeal to Millennials are having a significant impact on colleges. For example, new infrastructures are being implemented, and residence halls rooms must come cable-ready and connected to the Internet. As this connected generation continues to move into college, faculty, staff, and students themselves will have to establish new ways to capitalize on Millennials' desire to stay in touch.

Conclusion

History and popular culture are important determinants of a generation's values, beliefs, and behaviors. As Ortega y Gasset (1941) declares, "Man [sic], in a word, has not nature; what he has is. . . . history. . . . Man. . . . finds that he has no nature other than what he himself has done" (p. 217). What humankind has done is develop history and culture, and it becomes incumbent on those whose work it is to educate to understand both. Each generation has its own history, shaped in no small part by interaction with popular culture. Using history to understand the lives of students and tracking popular culture forms and trends will offer student affairs educators important tools for working with these students in the future.

References

Abrams, A. "They Called It the Me Decade." *Long Island/Queens Our Future: The 20th Century: A Look Back.* Retrieved Oct. 3, 2003, from http://future.newsday.com/century/8cov0830.htm.

Astin, A. W., and others. *Spirituality in College Students: Preliminary Findings from a National Study.* Los Angeles: Higher Education Research Institute, 2003.

Astin, A. W., Oseguera, L., Sax, L. J., and Korn, W. S. *The American Freshman: Thirty-Five Year Trends.* Los Angeles: Higher Education Research Institute, 2002.

Beaudoin, T. *Virtual Faith: The Irreverent Spiritual Quest of Generation X.* San Francisco: Jossey-Bass, 1998.

Brokaw, T. *The Greatest Generation.* New York: Random House, 1998.

Bronner, S. J. *Piled Higher and Deeper: The Folklore of Student Life.* Little Rock, Ark.: August House, 1990.

Brooks, K., Schiraldi, V., and Ziedenberg, J. *School House Hype: Two Years Later.* Washington, D.C.: Justice Policy Institute, 2000.

Carlson, S. "Napster Was Nothing Compared with This Year's Bandwidth Problems." *Chronicle of Higher Education,* 2001, Sept. 28, p. A44.

Carlson, S. "A President Tries to Settle the Controversy Over File Sharing." *Chronicle of Higher Education,* 2003, May 23, p. A27.

Cimino, R., and Lattin, D. *Shopping for Faith: American Religion in the New Millennium.* San Francisco: Jossey-Bass, 1998.

Coomes, M. D. "Student Financial Aid." In F.J.D. MacKinnon and Associates (eds.), *Rentz's Student Affairs Practice in Higher Education.* Springfield, Ill.: Charles C. Thomas, 2004.

Digital Bits. "CEA DVD Player Sales." 2003. Retrieved Sept. 23, 2003 from http://www.thedigitalbits.com/articles/cemadvdsales.html.

Dunn, J. "The Secret Life of Teenage Girls." *Rolling Stone,* Nov. 11, 1999, *825,* 106–108, 111–121.

Federal Election Commission. "Voter Registration and Turnout, 2000," n.d. Retrieved Apr. 22, 2004 from http://www.fec.gov/pages/2000turnout/reg&to00.htm.

Foroohar, R., and Itoi, K. "Don't Be Lame." *Newsweek,* Sept. 8, 2003, pp. E10-E11.

Friedman, T. L. "An Islamic Reformation." *New York Times,* Dec. 4, 2002, sect. A; p. 31.

Giroux, H. A. "Teenage Sexuality, Body Politics, and the Pedagogy of Display." In J. S. Epstein (ed.), *Youth Culture: Identity in a Postmodern Word.* Malden, Mass.: Blackwell, 1998.

Gorey, G. A. "Point of View: Steal This MP3 File." *Chronicle of Higher Education,* May 23, 2003, p. B20.

Graham, J. T. *Theory of History in Ortega y Gasset: "The Dawn of Historical Reason."* Columbia: University of Missouri Press, 1997.

Gripsrud, J. "'High Culture' Revisited." In J. Storey (ed.), *Cultural Theory and Popular Culture* (2nd ed.). Athens: University of Georgia Press, 1998.

"Impeachment and Beyond." *New York Times,* Dec. 20, 1998, sect. 4, p. 12.

Jones, S. *Let the Games Begin: Gaming Technology and Entertainment Among College Students.* Washington, D.C.: Pew Internet and American Life Project, 2003.

Kiernan, V. "Higher-Education Organizations Urge a Crackdown on Illegal File-Sharing." *Chronicle of Higher Education,* Oct. 25, 2002, p. A37.

Kitwana, B. *The Hip Hop Generation: Young Blacks and the Crisis in African-American Culture.* New York: BasicCivitas Books, 2002.

Kuh, G. D., and Whitt, E. J. *The Invisible Tapestry: Culture in American Colleges and Universities.* ASHE-ERIC Education Report, no. 1. Washington, D.C.: Association for the Study of Higher Education, 1998.

Levine, A. *When Dreams and Heroes Died: A Portrait of Today's College Student.* San Francisco: Jossey-Bass, 1981.

Lipsitz, G. "The Hip Hop Hearings: Censorship, Social Memory, and Intergenerational Tensions Among African Americans." In J. Austin and M. N. Willard (eds.), *Generations of Youth: Youth Cultures and History in Twentieth-Century America.* New York: New York University Press, 1998.

Mack, A. M. "Verizon Seeks New Way to Woo Teens." *Adweek: Midwest Edition,* Oct. 13, 2003, *44*(40), 13.

Magolda, P. M. "The Campus Tour: Ritual and Community in Higher Education." *Anthropology & Education Quarterly,* 2000, *31*(1), 24–46.

Magolda, P. M. "What Our Rituals Tell Us About Community on Campus: A Look at the Campus Tour." *About Campus,* 2001, *5*(6), 2–8.

Mangan, K. S. "U. of Texas Plans Workshops Devoted to Sexual Abstinence." *Chronicle of Higher Education.* Oct. 6, 1995.Retrieved October 7, 2003 from http://chronicle.com/prm/che-data/articles.dir/art-42.dir/issue-06.dir/06a04401.htm.

Manning, K. *Rituals, Ceremonies, and Cultural Meaning in Higher Education* (Critical Studies in Education and Culture Series, H. Giroux, series ed.). Westport, Conn.: Bergin and Garvey, 2000.

Marías, J. *Generations: A Historical Method* (H. C. Raley, trans.). Tuscaloosa: University of Alabama Press, 1967.

Morris, J. "Teens Driving the Cell Phone Market: The Allure Includes Colorful Accessories." *Union Leader,* Aug. 8, 2003, p. D1.

Nachbar, J., and Lause, K. "Getting to Know Us. An Introduction to the Study of Popular Culture: What Is This Stuff That Dreams Are Made of?" In J. Nachbar and K. Lause, *Popular Culture: An Introductory Text.* Bowling Green, Ohio: Bowling Green State University Popular Press, 1992.

Njubi, F. N. "Rap, Race, and Representation." In M. A. Oliker and W. P. Krolikowski, S.J. (eds.), *Images of Youth: Popular Culture as Educational Ideology.* New York: Peter Lang, 2001.

Ortega y Gasset, J. *History as a System and Other Essays Toward a Philosophy of History.* New York: Norton, 1941/1961.

Ortega y Gasset, J. *Mission of the University* (H. L. Nostrand, ed. and trans.). New York: Norton, 1992. (Originally published 1944)

Pew Research Center. "The 2004 Political Landscape: Evenly Divided and Increasingly Polarized." Nov.5, 2003. Retrieved Nov. 6, 2003 from http://people-press.org/reports/display.php3?ReportID=196.

Phillips, K. "On the Brink of Neo-Puritanism." *The Times Union,* Jan. 6, 1999, p. A9.

Rutenberg, J., "Survey Shows Few Parents Use TV V-Chip to Limit Children's Viewing." *New York Times,* July 25, 2001, sect. E, p. 1.

Sax, L. J., and others. *The American Freshman: National Norms for Fall 2002.* Los Angeles: Higher Education Research Institute, 2002.

Schein, E. H. *Organizational Culture and Leadership* (2nd ed.). San Francisco: Jossey-Bass, 1992.

Schlesinger Jr., A. M. *The Cycles of American History.* Boston: Houghton Mifflin, 1986.

"Secretary Shalala Unveils New Girl Power—Girl Scout Partnership." *Valley Views,* 1998, 5(2), 2–3.

Steinberg, N. *If at All Possible, Involve a Cow: The Book of College Pranks.* New York: St. Martin's Press, 1992.

Storey, J. (ed.). *Cultural Theory and Popular Culture* (2nd ed.). Athens: University of Georgia Press, 1998.

Strauss, W., and Howe, N. *Generations: The History of America's Future, 1584 to 2069.* New York: Morrow, 1991.

Strinati, D. *An Introduction to the Theories of Popular Culture.* New York: Routledge, 1995.

Tapscott, D. *Growing up Digital: The Rise of the Net Generation.* New York: McGraw-Hill, 1998.

Wolfe, T. "The Me Decade and the Third Awakening." *The Purple Decade: A Reader.* New York: Berkley Books, 1987. (Original work published 1976)

Wright, B. W. *Comic Book Nation: The Transformation of Youth Culture in America.* Baltimore, Md.: Johns Hopkins University Press, 2001.

Young, J. R. "Sssshhh. We're Taking Notes Here." *Chronicle of Higher Education,* Aug. 8, 2003, p. A29.

MICHAEL D. COOMES *is associate professor of higher education and student affairs at Bowling Green State University in Ohio.*

3

This chapter demonstrates how literature about Millennial students offers a view of some of the thematic elements that bring this generation into focus for educators who would appeal to these characteristics to help students learn, develop, and grow.

Millennials Coming to College

Robert DeBard

The first truth to acknowledge in trying to encapsulate the characteristics of Millennial students who are starting to matriculate through collegiate programs is that they are the most racially and ethnically diverse in this nation's history (Howe and Strauss, 2003; National Center for Education Statistics, 2000). According to figures released by the NCES (2000), between 1980, when the members of Generation X began to attend college, and 2000, when the Millennials began to attend college, enrollment of white students as a percentage of total decreased from 81.53 percent to 69.38 percent. Enrollment of women increased from 51.45 percent of the total to 56.12 percent. The number of Asian American students alone increased more than threefold, whereas overall enrollment in higher education grew only 22 percent.

Even if two-year college students are not factored into the comparison, new students attending this nation's four-year institutions display a changing demographic. When the annual Freshmen Survey of the Fall 2002 (Sax and others, 2002) is compared to that of five years before (fall 1998), first year students are less white (75.8 percent, down from 82.5 percent), wealthier (45.2 percent of parental income is above $75,000 per year, compared to 25.1 percent in 1998, with more than twice as many making over $100,000), and more ambitious (more than 75 percent of the first-year students surveyed indicated plans to pursue a degree beyond a bachelor's, compared to 66 percent five years before). Interestingly, in a recent statistical report issued by the National Household Education Program (NHEP) of 7,910 sixth through twelfth graders, fully 94 percent responded "yes" to the question "Do you think you will attend college?" Tellingly, 96 percent of their parents thought so (Horn, Chen, and Chapman, 2003). Still, the challenge is to recognize that demographic tendencies do not always capture reality. For instance, with regard to family wealth, although it can be reported that there are more wealthy parents, it also was reported that there are nearly as many families making $25,000 or below (14.1 percent) as compared to 1998 (14.8 percent). So the gap in earnings might be as informative to those working with students as any general characteristics about current family wealth of the parents of Millennial students.

Granting the diversity of this generation, research has also indicated that Millennial students coming to college have certain characteristics (Howe and Strauss, 2000; Lancaster and Stillman, 2002; Newton, 2000; Sax, 2003; Schneider and Stevenson, 1999; Zemke, Raines, and Filipczak, 2000). This chapter discusses these characteristics because they are important to understanding the expectations and motivations of Millennial students. It is also important to take into consideration how the characteristics of this generation interact with those of the Baby Boomer and Gen X generations who are now in faculty and administrative service roles in higher education. Such an understanding can help facilitate the education of these new students as well as yield information for their primarily Boomer-generation parents who view themselves as partners in the consumption of this service.

The Characteristics of Millennial College Students

Neil Howe and William Strauss have established themselves as the most often cited writers about the Millennial generation. Their works, beginning with *Generations: The History of America's Future 1584 to 2069* (Strauss and Howe, 1991); *13th Gen: Abort, Retry, Ignore, Fail?* (Howe and Strauss, 1993); *The Fourth Turning: An American Prophecy* (Strauss and Howe, 1997); and *Millennials Rising: The Next Great Generation* (Howe and Strauss, 2000), have explored the cyclical nature of the transitions between generations as well as the popular perceptions of and perspectives toward the more recent generations. The characteristics they have listed as core personality traits of the Millennial generation are commonly cited in the press, and these traits do seem to represent a compelling set of descriptors worth using in this text. However, there is an ironic caution that must be issued in using Howe and Strauss in this regard, one that they themselves have acknowledged. Being Boomer-generation parents of Millennial-generation children, their central optimistic premise that this will be the "next great generation" is all too typical of Boomer parents' description of them.

Parental pride notwithstanding, the list provided by Howe and Strauss (2000) can be used as a template against which other observers can be compared. It should be kept in mind that Howe and Strauss meant for these characteristics to include the views of, as well as toward, Millennial students. This is important because it demonstrates a cyclical aspect of culture: if people are treated in such a way as to reinforce behavior as part of normative expectations, they tend to believe this behavior represents who they are and what is expected of them and their peers (Schein, 1992; Smircich,

1983). Boomer-generation authority figures in Millennial students' lives have created an environmental press of rewards and sanctions that have provided for and reinforced certain preferred normative behaviors helping these generational characteristics to emerge (Brooks, 2001). What follows is a set of characteristics identified by Howe and Strauss (2000) that does furnish a sense of perspective on the central tendencies of Millennial-generation college students.

Special. The first trait, being "special," is in response to boomer authority figures telling members of the Millennial generation all their lives that they are special. Perhaps because of their numbers, projected to be between seventy-six and ninety million depending on immigration trends (Howe and Strauss, 2003) and the relative wealth of their parents, Millennials have been made to feel important by those, including colleges and universities, who would sell them a product or service. They have been made to feel vital to their parents' sense of purpose. Indeed, one of the ancillary aspects of serving Millennial students is dealing constructively with their intrusive parents (Shapiro, 2002). As children, they were given trophies for participation rather than victory. According to the Howe and Strauss theory of generational types (Strauss and Howe, 1991), Millennials are considered to be a "civic" generation. As a civic generation they perceived coming-of-age as "good" and "empowering," as opposed to the "reactive" peer personality of Generation X, who, these authors asserted, perceived coming-of-age as "bad" and "alienating" (p. 365). Going along with this theory, as Millennials move into adulthood they will identify with "building"; in fact, one of the descriptors of this generation is "the builders." It follows not only that these students are to be considered special by those who would provide for their student service needs because of the high expectations placed on them but also that they would perceive themselves as special and highly expectant.

Sheltered. One primary way that authority figures have displayed how special Millennial children are is to shelter them from harm's way—evident from "baby on board" signs and child safety rules to post-Columbine name tags and lockdown schools. Millennials have been encouraged to follow the rules, and they also have come to expect the rules to be clearly communicated and enforced with due process (Martin and Tulgan, 2001). In short, for educators and service providers it had best be in the syllabus or policy handbook if it is to be enforced.

One of the ironies of this generational interplay has been that Baby Boomers who lived by the mantra of "unconditional amnesty" have imposed upon the Millennials policies calling for zero tolerance (Howe and Strauss, 2000). This has resulted in a need for and expectation of structure on the part of Millennial students. Parents of Millennials have organized their children's lives to give direction; this effort has been supported by day care options, after-school programs, recreational centers, music and dance lessons, and arts programs that have come to occupy an increasing amount of what was formerly free play time for this nation's youth (Howe and Strauss, 2000). The end result is that Millennials have come both to trust authority and to count on authority. Schneider and Stevenson (1999) entitled their book on Millennial generation teenagers *The Ambitious Generation: America's Teenagers, Motivated but Directionless* because they found Millennial teenagers tended to have high ambitions but no clear life plan. These teenagers also tend to overestimate the amount of education they will need for a chosen career path and have chosen an educational route with low odds of success. Obviously, this is all conjecture, but it does bring up the question of whether being sheltered has superimposed direction that could result in college students being directionless when they are liberated by the college environment.

Confident. The trait of confidence involves just what Millennials have come to expect of their future. A sense of optimism is related to the generally high degree of confidence possessed by this generation of students. Millennials have come to expect good news and have been encouraged to believe in themselves (Lancaster and Stillman, 2002). This has been nurtured through awards and rewards for what the authority figures in their lives judge to be good behavior. From trophies for agreeing to participate in activities as children to scholarship grants for passing proficiency tests in high school, Millennials have tended to trust this authority because it has worked on their behalf. Partly because of their civic orientation and partly because of their practical approach to achieving outcomes, they believe in community service as long as they get credit for it, literally and figuratively (Zemke, Raines, and Filipczak, 2000).

This generation seems to have mastered the art of negotiating levels of acceptable behavior with parents, teachers, and even employers (Zemke, Raines, and Filipczak, 2000). They are confident of their ability to match the effort required to meet the expectations others place upon them and are motivated to do so as long as their own expectations of beneficial outcomes are met.

Conventional. A characteristic that the positive thesis of Howe and Strauss would advance to counter Schneider and Stevenson's fear that Millennials have been so protected that many of its members have become "directionless dreamers" is that Millennial students are highly conventional. Millennials have come to accept the social rules that have been imposed upon them because the Boomer authority figures who have defined the rules also have the power and resources to support such good behavior by supporting those who follow convention. This has resulted in Millennials respecting cultural differences far more than the Boomer authority figures do, who in turn have encouraged them to do so. There is a considerable amount of "do as we say, not as we did" interaction between Millennial students and Boomer authority figures (Howe and Strauss, 2000). Millennials have come to accept codes of conduct and dress. They have come to expect high-stakes proficiency testing as a rite of passage (DeBard and Kubow, 2002).

Even though there has been some movement on the part of college freshmen, who, when surveyed, increasingly identify themselves as politically liberal or politically conservative rather than independent, it has been suggested that this could be tied to the assumed stance of those Boomer adults who have such influence on them (Sax, 2003). Indeed, the latest Cooperative Institutional Research Program (CIRP) data from 2002 reflect how responsive this generation of college freshmen can be to authority. In reversing the five-year trend in which students gravitated toward politically liberal labels, there was some movement back to "middle of the road" or conservative leanings that have been ascribed to the events of September 11 and the popularity of President Bush at the time the survey was administered (Sax, 2003). Millennial students have learned that one of the best ways of getting along is to go along.

Team-Oriented. There is little question that the preponderance of Millennials want to get along by being team-oriented. Whether facilitated through the use of cell phones to keep in contact with friends and family, or by living-learning centers in residence halls to give thematic reinforcement for a sense of mission, Millennials like to congregate. Part of the motivation for this is their desire to cooperate and be perceived as being cooperative by those who are in a position to judge them (Howe and Strauss, 2000; Lancaster and Stillman, 2002). The imposition of rules and structure on them has certainly encouraged compliance as opposed to risk taking (Lancaster and Stillman, 2002).

Still, these students do seem more upbeat about working with each other on projects. In fact, there is some resentment when they are forced to compete in a zero-sum game where losers walk away empty-handed (Murray, 1997). It should not be surprising that win-win conflict mediation has engendered expectations that cooperation leads to beneficial resolution. Being a member of a team lowers the pressure on individuals. On the job, Millennials tend to like collective action. As students, they enjoy working on academic project teams.

The downside can be that Millennial students expect such actions and projects to be highly structured because they do not like to work without a net (Howe and Strauss, 2000). It has been suggested that, when they do encounter difficult people, they become uncomfortable and expect those in authority to protect them (Lancaster and Stillman, 2002). However, they are highly motivated by noble causes and readily volunteer to join with a group of their peers, as long as there are Boomer mentors who are there to make sure the cause is achievable (Sax, 2003).

Achieving. There is also no doubt that one of the primary characteristics of the Millennial generation members is their need for achievement. Millennials expect to be held accountable, if this accountability can be achieved through good behavior. A lack of tolerance for aberrant behavior is acceptable as long as the rewards for conventional behavior are known to all (Martin and Tulgan, 2001). One residual effect of high-stakes testing is this generation's respect for objective assessment, as opposed to subjective evaluation (Kubow and DeBard, 2002). The concept of "fair" should be criteria-based in their view, not subject to idiosyncratic interpretation and white, male bias.

Millennial children have seen their mothers and other women in their lives make massive strides during this generation's lifetime and are both optimistic and expectant that meritocratic ascension will be part of their adult life (Sax and others, 2002). More than twice as many college freshmen, reported in the CIRP data, expect to earn at least a B average in college, compared to twenty years ago, and 61.2 percent of women believe so compared to only 49.7 percent in 1998. The number of first-year women students who project that they will earn a bachelor's degree has increased from 68.9 percent in 1998 to 81.8 percent in 2002. They are willing to invest in higher education, but they also expect those in authority (parents, institutional officials, politicians) to invest in them (Horn, Chen, and Chapman, 2003).

These Millennial students have high respect for "heroes" created by the media, particularly those who lead others through the valley to the summit (Sax, 2003). Furthermore, they dream of being able to do the same. They have come to expect high grades as a reward for compliance to academic standards. Alignment of curriculum is to be matched by alignment of a reward structure that is clearly explained and cleanly administered.

Pressured. The final characteristic, being pressured, ties into this need for clarity in that Millennial students feel pressured to perform; they want a structure enforced to ensure that compliance will lead to achievement. They have been pushed by their Boomer parents to be the best that they can be in order to help demonstrate how good Baby Boom parenting has been. They have been made to feel that Boomer parents, coaches, and leaders— for the sake of Millennial achievement—have created the many opportunities afforded them. They have been given trophies for competing, but their accomplishments represent trophies to those adults who would take credit for these accomplishments. The end result is pressure to perform at least, and excel at best.

This characteristic has led to the Millennials' reliance on structure. They have come to trust that their elders will organize a path toward success as long as these young people do not divert from it. There is a respect for conformity because it relieves the pressure to improvise (Howe and Strauss, 2000). Millennials feel enough pressure to conform to the expectations that have been codified for them through zero tolerance policies and standardized performance measurements without also having to be creative.

Comparing Generational Values

The environment for Millennial students coming to college would seem to be fairly accommodating as long as all their student peers were traditionally aged and those who teach and serve them were Boomers. Of course, such is not the case. Aside from the reality that prevalent characteristics do not capture all Millennials, particularly those students who can be described as "at risk" (Hu and St. John, 2001) or nontraditional students (Aslanian, 2001), the mixture of Boomer and Generation X faculty and staff makes for a very complex environmental equation.

One of the great challenges to Millennial students in college is to navigate the turbulent water of divergent values practiced and espoused by those who do not share the characteristics ascribed to Millennials (Lancaster and Stillman, 2002). Although Howe and Strauss again lead the way in such intergenerational comparison, several other observers have written about these differences.

It is important to acknowledge that students learn, develop, and grow within a context of imprints that nurture or stifle potential values and subsequent behavior that is aligned with them. Anthropologists tend to attribute the evolution of societies to cultural rituals, artifacts, and symbols to guide those who would become accepted into a culture. Sociologists tend to view the environmental press that pushes individuals and groups in directions in order to oppress options or liberate them, depending on the dominant power structure within the society. Psychologists invest more in individual ability to make sense out of this external environment by taking control of internal perceptions. The emergence of values is a common concern of all of these fields of study. As we reviewed in Chapter One, Millennial students have been influenced by the generations that came before them. They have been made to respond to an environmental press constructed by those in authority, and they have been challenged to be the greatest and happiest generation as a result of their individual abilities and values (Howe and Strauss, 2000).

One way to compare values is to develop a list of collective views or perceptual categories and then indicate how the generation cohorts would tend to thematically respond to these prompts (see Table 3.1). By so doing, it is possible to come to appreciate the differences between the generations that are currently occupying the vast majority of the higher education environment. This comparison can depict some of the flash points of potential conflict between Boomers, Gen Xers and Millennials as well as give some indication as to how these conflicts can be reconciled in order to better serve the current generation of students winding their way through institutions of higher learning.

Table 3.1 represents a compilation of twelve descriptors, used variously by Howe and Strauss (2000), as part of their theory of generational cycles; by Zemke, Raines, and Filipczak (2000), as they described potential conflicts within the work setting; and by Lancaster and Stillman (2002), as they described what they call "clashpoints" between Boomers, Gen Xers and Millennial workers.

In analyzing the importance of such a table of differing characteristics, the issue is how these values might play themselves out on campus as

Table 3.1. Comparing Generation Values

Views Toward	Boomers	Gen Xers	Millennials
Level of trust	Confident of self, not authority	Low toward authority	High toward authority
Loyalty to institutions	Cynical	Considered naive	Committed
Most admire	Taking charge	Creating enterprise	Following a hero of integrity
Career goals	Build a stellar career	Build a portable career	Build parallel careers
Rewards	Title and the corner office	Freedom not to do	Meaningful work
Parent-child involvement	Receding	Distant	Intruding
Having children	Controlled	Doubtful	Definite
Family life	Indulged as children	Alienated as children	Protected as children
Education	Freedom of expression	Pragmatic	Structure of accountability
Evaluation	Once a year with documentation	"Sorry, but how am I doing?"	Feedback whenever I want it
Political orientation	Attack oppression	Apathetic, individual	Crave community
The big question	What does it mean?	Does it work?	How do we build it?

Boomer and Generation X faculty and staff work with Millennial students. One trend that the CIRP freshmen survey responses have displayed is that lax academic standards in high school are a part of the Millennial experience, despite indications that academic standards are tightening (Sax, 2003). It could be that requirements are tightening, but according to the 2002 survey the proportion of students earning an A average in high school reached 45.7 percent, compared to 17.6 back in 1968, and the number earning a grade of C or lower dropped to 5.3 percent, compared to 23.1 percent in 1968.

The bind that this creates for educators is that, on the one hand, Millennial students have come to expect high grades as a way of validating their achievement; on the other, they will only do what is expected of them to achieve these outcomes (Sax, 2003). In her chapter on "Teaching, Learning, and Millennial Students" in this volume, Wilson considers some of the implications of this dichotomy between high aspirations and low expectations. Suffice it to say, for the intention of this chapter, that nurturing the self-esteem of Millennial students is common for Boomers in authority positions. As Sax (2003) has written, "Whatever the reason behind the escalation in students' grades, its effect appears to be clear: students have grown increasingly optimistic about their chances for academic success in college" (p. 17).

Certainly optimism is a characteristic that has been trumpeted as a strength of this generation. The problem is that the CIRP survey also found that the percentage of students who devote six or more hours per week to studying or homework declined to an all-time low of 33.4 percent in 2002, compared to a high of 47 percent when the question was first asked on the 1987 survey. Such optimism, when not supported by effort, can be a source of conflict, particularly with members of Generation X, who feel less sanguine about their own treatment as a generation whose reputation for achievement has been challenged (Lancaster and Stillman, 2002).

Another area of potential challenge in providing services to Millennial students involves their *practice* of work versus their view of work. It is clear that they desire to have a positive impact on people as well as to work at a job that holds meaning for them (Lancaster and Stillman, 2002; Zemke, Raines, and Filipczak, 2000). The problem is that, as they attempt to reach these goals through attainment of a college education, more pragmatic concerns about employment come into play. When all undergraduates are factored into the equation, more than three out of four college students are currently working an average of thirty-one hours per week while attending college (National Center for Education Statistics, 1998). The fact that as of 1998 47 percent of full-time students were working compared to 34 percent in 1970 has implications for those who would encourage student engagement on campus (Kuh, 2003). Since the vast majority of student employment is off campus, this runs counter to the advice from Astin (1993) in his research on degree attainment, campus involvement, and student satisfaction with the collegiate experience. This situation does not appear to be getting better. According to the CIRP data (Sax and others, 2002), a record 47.1 percent of four-year college freshmen expect to take jobs in order to finance their college education. This employment practice might help explain why, despite their seemingly good intentions, Millennial students' study habits do not on average keep pace with their ambitions (Sax, 2003; Schneider and Stevenson, 1999). Boomer faculty are self-absorbed enough to believe that an assignment is an obligation. They are willing to use their belief in competition to sort out high achievers from the merely ambitious (Howe and Strauss, 2000). It has become fashionable to speak of learner-centered classrooms (Barr and Tagg, 1995), but the expectations of Boomer professors will not let performance evaluation become a point of negotiation.

Time limitations can also cause conflict between the value Millennials place on volunteerism and service learning and the actual practice of this value. Sax (2003) has pointed out that circumstances can be highly disruptive to a student's ability to do meaningful volunteer work or engage in service learning activities. Millennial students have become used to receiving rewards for service in high school and tend to carry this expectation into college. Such strategies as providing a stipend for students who assume leadership roles on campus or academic credit for groups of students who conduct service learning projects might be justified and are an inherent part of the Millennial mind-set, but they tend to encourage compliance rather than commitment (Sax, 2000).

The pragmatic approach Millennial students tend to take toward curricular requirements and extracurricular opportunities on their campus can be related to their ambition. Members of this generation aim to please, as long as it promises to advance their goals to raise a family in a dual-income professional household. The educational attainment goals of Millennials are the highest ever surveyed. Higher education advocates have been so successful in persuading Millennial students of the need for a college diploma that almost half of the teenagers studied hope to get a degree that exceeds the credentials needed for their desired field or occupation (Schneider and Stevenson, 1999). Additionally, the rate at which tenth and twelfth graders expect to enter certain occupations is much greater than the actual prevalence of these jobs as projected for 2005 (Schneider and Stevenson, 1999). It is also a reality of the Millennial generation's ambition that the educational aspirations of students in two-year institutions have increased dramatically over the last twenty years (Aslanian, 2001).

The flashpoint of conflict has not yet been seen within institutions, but the impending onslaught of retirees from the Baby Boom generation could strain the economic resources expected to be generated by the college-educated Millennial generation workers. The resulting clash between high expectations on the part of both generations could cause social strain (Lancaster and Stillman, 2002).

A final point of potential conflict of values involves the supposed respect for authority and loyalty to institutions attributed to Millennial students. It has been pointed out that students are aware of campus and community regulations and political correctness but are determined to find a way around them, create the right appearance by hiding unapproved behavior, and live by a philosophy of "it's OK as long as I don't get caught" (Newton, 2000). Academic honesty does seem to be an issue with these students (Sax and others, 2002). Their technological savvy and access to information, undreamed of by Boomers when they were winding their way through research papers and reports in college, are a temptation in which achievement is put up against integrity. Plagiarism is the most serious of academic misbehaviors, but the pressure to achieve desired outcomes can blur the ethics for the overly ambitious.

Conclusion

The characteristics of Millennial-generation college students are, as one might expect, a mixed bag. Sax (2003) asserted, on the basis of CIRP data, that "compared to students just five or six years ago, today's freshmen are more academically optimistic, service-oriented, and politically engaged. They also have less experience with alcohol and cigarettes than their recent counterparts" (p. 19). However, she went on to point out that they are studying less than ever before, are working more off campus, and are less committed to working on important issues such as the environment and race relations. There is also some concern that high school grade inflation, combined with a decrease in study time, might be setting Millennial students up for unrealistic expectations for what it takes to succeed academically and to prepare themselves professionally (Schneider and Stevenson, 1999).

For all that, there is no denying that Millennial students have the numbers to dominate both the educational scene and economic reality for the preceding generations, as Gen Xers move into midlife and Boomers into elderhood. Despite some concerns about academic honesty, they do tend to follow the rules, as long as they are vigilantly enforced and well explained. The reminder of this volume addresses some of the specific implications of these characteristics for higher education in general and student affairs practitioners in particular.

Neil Howe and William Strauss found the young people they surveyed for their book *Millennials Rising* (2000) to be generally a hardworking, cheerful, earnest, and deferential group. However, because student affairs practitioners know that life is sometimes messy more than organized, stressful more than balanced, and full of disappointment as well as promise, the Millennials have characteristics that are at once enjoyable and challenging. The need for competent practice to meet Millennial students' aspirations and Millennial parents' expectations should keep the student affairs profession well occupied for years to come.

References

Aslanian, C. *Adult Students Today.* New York: College Board, 2001.

Astin, A. W. *What Matters in College? Four Critical Years Revisited.* San Francisco: Jossey-Bass, 1993.

Barr, R. B., and Tagg, J. "From Teaching to Learning: A New Paradigm for Undergraduate Education." *Change,* 1995, 27(6), 12–25.

Brooks, D. "The Organization Kid." *Atlantic Monthly,* April 2001, 287(4), 40–54.

DeBard, R., and Kubow, P. K. "From Compliance to Commitment: The Need for Constituent Discourse in Implementing Testing Policy." *Educational Policy,* 2002, 3, 387–405.

Horn, L. J., Chen, X., and Chapman, C. *Getting Ready to Pay for College: What Students and Their Parents Know About the Cost of College Tuition and What They Are Doing to Find out* (NCES report no. 2003–030). Washington, D.C.: National Center for Education Statistics, 2003.

Howe, N., and Strauss, W. *13th Gen: Abort, Retry, Ignore, Fail?* New York: Vintage Books, 1993.

Howe, N., and Strauss, W. *Millennials Rising: The Next Great Generation.* New York: Vintage Books, 2000.

Howe, N., and Strauss, W. *Millennials Go to College.* Great Falls, Va.: American Association of Registrars and Admissions Officers and LifeCourse Associates, 2003.

Hu, S., and St. John, E. P. "Student Persistence in a Public Higher Education System: Understanding Racial and Ethnic Differences." *Journal of Higher Education,* 2001, 72(3), 265–286.

Kubow, P. K., and DeBard, R. *From Proficiency to Authenticity: A Holistic School Development and Assessment Plan.* New York: Nova Science, 2002.

Kuh, G. D. "What We're Learning About Student Engagement from NSSE." *Change,* 2003, 35(2), 24–32.

Lancaster, L. C., and Stillman, D. *When Generations Collide: Who They Are. Why They Clash. How to Solve the Generational Puzzle at Work.* New York: HarperBusiness, 2002.

Martin, C. A., and Tulgan, B. *Managing Generation Y.* New Haven, Conn.: HRD Press, 2001.

Murray, N. D. "Welcome to the Future: The Millennial Generation." *Journal of Career Planning and Employment,* 1997, 57(3), 36–40.

National Center for Education Statistics. *Postsecondary Financing Strategies: How Undergraduates Combine Work, Borrowing, and Attendance.* Washington, D.C.: U. S. Department of Education, 1998.

National Center for Education Statistics. *The Condition of Education, 2000.* Washington, D.C.: U.S. Department of Education, 2000.

Newton, F. B. "The New Student." *About Campus,* 2000, 5(5), 8–15.

Sax, L. J. "Citizenship Development and the American College Student." In T. Ehrlich (ed.), *Higher Education and Civic Responsibility.* Phoenix, Ariz.: Oryx Press, 2000.

Sax, L. J. "Our Incoming Students: What Are They Like?" *About Campus,* 2003, 8(3), 15–20.

Sax, L. J., and others. *The American Freshman: National Norms for Fall 2002.* Los Angeles: Higher Education Research Institute, 2002.

Schein, E. H. *Organizational Culture and Leadership* (2nd ed.). San Francisco: Jossey-Bass, 1992.

Schneider, B., and Stevenson, D. *The Ambitious Generation: America's Teenagers, Motivated But Directionless.* New Haven, Conn.: Yale University Press, 1999.

Shapiro, J. R. "Keeping Parents off Campus." *New York Times,* Aug. 22, 2002, p. 23.

Smircich, L. "Concepts of Culture and Organizational Analysis." *Administrative Science Quarterly,* 1983, 28, 39–58.

Strauss, W., and Howe, N. *Generations: The History of America's Future, 1584 to 2069.* New York: Morrow, 1991.

Strauss, W., and Howe, N. *The Fourth Turning: An American Prophecy.* New York: Broadway Books, 1997.

Zemke, R., Raines, C., and Filipczak, R. *Generations at Work: Managing the Clash of Veterans, Boomers, Xers, and Nexters in Your Workplace.* New York: AMACOM, 2000.

ROBERT DEBARD is associate professor of higher education and student affairs and interim director of the School of Leadership and Policy Studies at Bowling Green State University in Ohio.

4

This chapter explores the dynamics of generational cohort differences and their potential influence on the understandings, emphases, and applications of student development theory.

Constructions of Student Development Across the Generations

C. Carney Strange

The idea that generational cohort differences might shape how we construct and explain the dynamics of human development is certainly not new to educators. One need only point, for example, to the importance of conventions and norms for the GI generation (born between 1901 and 1924) in establishing clear guidelines as to what was considered "normal" and "customary"; they defined the essential role of the intact family and other social institutions in nurturing its young along the path to early adulthood. Whether it came in the form of popular television shows ("Ozzie and Harriet," "Father Knows Best") or other cultural artifacts, the GI generation cohort contributed much to an understanding that learning, growth, and development was a normative experience with a clear set of maturation criteria supported by values, assumptions, and beliefs in "doing what is right." Alignment with these conventions was evidence enough that development had progressed along the correct path. Consequently, deviance was relegated to the abnormal and at best was symptomatic of maladjustment or immaturity. Thus from this Civic generational type (and its subsequent Silent generation cohort, born between 1924 and 1942) came notions of psychological maturity and advancement rooted deeply in conformity to the norm. An expected order was sought everywhere, and everyone had a place.

If the rallying cry of the GI and Silent generations is "We are!" then perhaps the claim most common to the Baby Boomers (born between 1943 and 1960) is "I am!" Rather than an emphasis on conventions and norms, in this particular era an emerging body of literature (for example, Chickering, 1969; Erikson, 1950; Keniston, 1965) began to focus on rejection of authority and the importance of individuation in the maturation process, as psychologists and educators sought to describe and understand the "breaking away" phenomenon in our culture. Endorsement of a "do your own thing" ethic led to constructions of learning, growth, and development that soon emphasized uniqueness, individuality, and independence, rather than conformity, as benchmarks of maturity. Questions of personal identity and fulfillment became paramount as educational and social institutions attempted to respond to a youth cohort bent on having its say and resisting confinement to any prescribed roles and expectations. What was once thought to bring comfort (that is, norms and conventions) was seen increasingly by many observers as a barrier to growth, and as constructions of human development changed so too did our practices. From homes and schools to churches and workplaces, freedom of choice and permissiveness defined what was appropriate, and a generation began its "voyage to the interior" (Gitlin, 1987) in a "culture of narcissism" (Lasch, 1979), laying the way for the next generation's immersion in identity and its dimensions of difference.

If being an *individual* highlights our understanding of human development during the Boomer era, being *different* may be what characterizes our explanation of those associated with Generation X (born between 1961 and 1981). The feminist and racial equality movements that took root in the 1960s bore much fruit by the time this subsequent generation came of age in the 1970s and 1980s. In the literature on student development, in particular, insights on various unique dimensions of identity underscored the idea that learning, growth, and development, rather than being normative, is a very different experience depending on personal characteristics such as race, ethnicity, gender, age, and sexual orientation. Authors such as Gilligan (1982), Cross (1995), Levinson (1978), and Cass (1979), for example, suggested that these characteristics and traits had been too long absent in accounts of the human experience, including definitions of maturity and the paths that appear to lead to it. In their critique, notions of normalcy were exposed as extensions of power and privilege supported by a dominant culture that favored the young, Caucasian, male, and heterosexual as the model of achievement and success. Constructions of learning, growth, and development were extended to new questions: Do members of an underrepresented culture (as defined, for example, by race or sexual orientation) progress differently on their path of identity development as a result of their interaction with the press of a dominant culture? Do factors such as gender and age accompany socialization processes that result in different patterns of interests and approaches to learning? These and other such questions have yielded more complex and inclusive theories in our repertoire that chart various nuances of human development and incorporate many of the myriad influences that have proven to shape the human experience.

In summary, a generational theory of human development would suggest that various emphases characteristic of a particular historic cohort set up expectations and standards that in turn shape not only the behavior of succeeding generation members but also how the current generation explains the course of development itself. With the front edge of the Millennial generation (born since 1981) now appearing on college and university campuses, the questions once again are raised: What distinguishes this emerging cohort from previous generations? How will its collective characteristics potentially shape our explanation of the dynamics and processes of student development?

By all accounts it appears that, with the rise of the Millennial generation in particular, theories about the learning, growth, and development of students may well turn to a new emphasis on the exocentric and relational aspects of the human experience. If previous generations are recognized by their respective claims of "we are" (GIs and Silents), "I am" (Boomers), and "we differ" (Generation X), several key purported features of the Millennials promise to reshape our thoughts around yet another new claim: "We connect!" Before examining this hypothesis, though, it is important to understand some of the fundamentals of the current student development theory base that might be challenged with the advent of this up-and-coming generation.

Current Models of Student Development

Over the past few decades, higher education and student affairs professionals have drawn from a wealth of theories and models in the student development literature, mapping out various progressions of learning, growth, and development during the college years. This body of understandings has accompanied a transformation of the field in recent years, focusing its attention on student learning (American College Personnel Association, 1994) and the potential of out-of-class opportunities for contributing to such an outcome (Kuh and others, 1991). Tenets that make up this knowledge base have served further to guide many campus policies and practices (Strange, 1994) and have challenged educators at all levels to reconsider the nature and design of campus learning environments (Strange and Banning, 2001).

Grounding this understanding are insights and constructs from three distinctive literatures, attending respectively to three fundamental aspects of student development: psychosocial-identity formation; evolution of cognitive-developmental meaning-making structures; and the emergence of personal preferences, styles, and types. Each stream of thought has contributed significantly to an understanding of the processes of human development and maturation during the college years, and each is likely to be influenced by the changing characteristics associated with this new generation of Millennial students.

Psychosocial-Identity Formation. Psychosocial-identity models chart human development through cycles of stability and transition across the life span, with particular attention to the dynamics of individuation and attachment. These models further identify age-appropriate developmental tasks reflective of maturation at various points in the life span. The works of Chickering and Reisser (1993), Neugarten (1968), Erikson (1950), and Levinson and Levinson (1996), for example, all address human development from such a perspective.

During a period of stability, closure is sought, firm choices are made, and life proceeds in response to a framework of expected relational and occupational commitments. In contrast, during a period of transition, questions are paramount, and previous life structures must be terminated, evaluated, and considered for inclusion in (or exclusion from) a subsequent new life structure. It is out of the ebb and flow of this cycle that questions of personal identity present themselves in powerful ways through various opportunities and choices. Predictably, such moments include processes of individuation (or "coming into one's own") and attachment (that is, affiliating with significant others). Furthermore, negotiation of these processes is shaped significantly, for example, by characteristics of gender, culture and ethnicity, and sexual orientation, inasmuch as such differences offer important contexts for the formation of personal identity.

The works of Atkinson, Morten, and Sue (1983), Josselson (1987), Gilligan (1982), Cross (1995), and Cass (1979) are exemplars of this line of inquiry focusing on the context of group identity. The further layering of psychosocial development with the dynamics of minority status in these models suggests that the development of a healthy self-concept is inescapably involved with the development of a positive cultural identity. Since concepts and assumptions of "normalcy" are inevitably products of the dominant culture, individuals who do not participate fully in that culture nor share its values are challenged most by a press toward conformity within two disparate cultures: one (a subculture) that acknowledges and supports their identities as members of a minority group; and another, a much larger and dominant group, that challenges their identities for their failure to match common expectations and norms (Strange and Banning, 2001). Neglect of the subculture removes an important source of support; neglect of the dominant culture might result in barriers to achievement. In effect, for these individuals success often entails a dual existence, capable of sustaining both the minority and the dominant cultures. Consequently, issues and tasks of development may be accompanied by additional degrees of stress and difficulty.

Cognitive Developmental Structures. The literature on cognitive structural development maps out patterns of meaning making that individuals bring to life experiences. Exemplifying this perspective, for example, are the works of Perry (1968), Kohlberg (1976), Gilligan (1982), Baxter Magolda (1992), and King and Kitchener (1994). According to these models, individuals progress through a stepwise, hierarchical sequence of stages or positions, each succeeding level characterized by greater complexity and qualitatively different assumptions about how things work with respect to a given domain. Early simplistic assumptions are gradually replaced by more advanced assumptions, as individuals seek new meanings for the events and experiences in their lives. For instance, in the domain of intellectual reasoning, individuals progress through increasingly complex forms (or stages) of reasoning as they advance in their ability to resolve problems of an "ill-structured" nature, with reference to experts in the field, to the compelling quality of available evidence, and to established rules of inquiry (King and Kitchener, 1994). Thus a person holding assumptions characteristic of early stages of reasoning might argue that the "truth value" of one point of view is established unquestionably by endorsement of an authority, or simply because one "believes it to be so," acknowledging that all points of view are equally valid since "no one knows for sure." At more advanced stages, though, a person acknowledges the difference between facts, opinions, and interpretations, reflecting a more complex understanding of inquiry as an inherently fallible process of critical review over a period of time, involving many sources of input from many individuals and yielding solutions that only approximate truth.

Figuring prominently in these descriptions of human development is the role of external power, authority, and expertise. Successful progression through advancing stages of meaning making is dependent on the capacity to move beyond the simple stability and comfort of certainty toward a complexity of unknowns and ambiguities. By definition, this involves rejection of external sources of knowing along the way, as a prelude to the development of a sense of self-authorship (Baxter Magolda, 1999) capable of critical consideration, decision making, and understanding. Lack of opportunities to encounter differences or to assume responsibility for judgment making attenuates this evolution and renders individuals with limited capabilities for understanding and managing complex phenomena.

Personal Preferences, Styles, and Types. The literature on personal preferences, styles, and types suggests that maturation is influenced by and expressed through relatively stable patterns that characterize how individuals approach and resolve the various tasks and challenges of learning, growth, and development. These theories underscore the importance of concurrent differences among individuals and how such differences reveal themselves in consistent ways in which they approach a variety of tasks. Models that illustrate this idea describe styles or patterns of behavior with respect to a variety of dimensions in students' lives, such as their vocational interests (Holland, 1973), personal styles (Myers, 1980), or learning orientations (Kolb, 1983). From such a perspective, individuals appear predictable as others recognize their "usual way of doing things." For example, we have learned how various "Myers-Briggs types" exhibit preferred ways of using "their minds, specifically the way they perceive and the way they make judgments" (Myers, 1980, p. 1). Some perceive primarily through the senses, whereas others rely upon intuition; some use a logical process of thinking to arrive at judgments, whereas others judge out of their appreciation and feelings for the event or situation. According to the model, either kind of perception can team up with either kind of judgment. Furthermore, depending on individuals' relative interest in their outer world (extraversion) or inner world (introversion), as well as their preference for a perceptive versus a judging attitude, a variety of combinations emerge reflecting "different kind[s] of personality, characterized by [differing] interests, values, needs, habits of mind, and surface traits" (Myers, 1980, p. 4). An important implication of these perspectives on human differences is that individuals develop relatively stable and consistent styles of performance over time that benefit from being taken into account when designing educational practice.

In summary, the student development literature thus far portrays college students as persons who are engaged in a variety of age-related developmental tasks; who construct meaning from and approach challenges of learning in characteristic patterns or styles; and who must resolve issues of individuation within the dynamics of gender, ethnicity, sexual orientation, and other identifying characteristics.

Millennial Implications for Student Development

The premise of this analysis is that each generational cohort brings a distinctive and characteristic emphasis to the human experience that translates into how members describe and understand the processes of learning, growth, and development. Thus, just as earlier generations in their own time have emphasized conventionality, individuality, or various identity differences in questions of maturation, the rising Millennial generation is also likely to draw attention to select features that will emerge from its own defining characteristics. These characteristics in turn might call into question some of the longstanding assumptions about how individuals learn, develop, and grow in our culture. They might also challenge some of the customary practices and procedures we have come to rely on in attending to their developmental needs.

Beginning with the entering class of the fall of 2000, a "group unlike any other youth generation in living memory" (Howe and Strauss, 2000, p. 4) entered the American higher education scene for the first time. Dubbed the Millennials, this cohort already appears "more numerous, more affluent, better educated, and more ethnically diverse" than previous generations and is "beginning to manifest a wide array of positive social habits. . . . including a new focus on teamwork, achievement, modesty, and good conduct" (p. 4). Over the next decade, some observers claim, "the Millennial Generation will entirely recast the image of youth from downbeat and alienated to upbeat and engaged—with potentially seismic consequences" (p. 4). Being optimistic and cooperative team players, accepting of authority, rule followers, and smarter than most think, the Millennials "represent a sharp break from Generation X, and are running exactly counter to trends launched by the Boomers" (p. 7). Having been nurtured

with a collective sense of being special, they are a "watched-over" generation, with the confidence to succeed in response to their "trophy kid" pressure to excel. As a *Civic* generation (Strauss and Howe, 1991), these youths
support convention—the idea that rules can help. Although healthier than
most previous generations, they also bring with them higher incidences of
asthma, obesity, and attention deficit hyperactivity disorder, exemplars of
a range of health and safety risks that "have all been directly and credibly
linked to the more structured, regimented, and indoor lifestyle of today's
children and teens—a lifestyle that results in less free play at recess, less
unsupervised exercise, and less unorganized outdoor activity" (p. 94). What
are the implications of these features, if borne out, for how we might recon-
struct the course of student development during the college years? What
are the implications for how we might respond to this generation's needs in
our educational policies and practices?

As explicated in Chapter Three, and supported by a compilation of
authors, seven defining characteristics seem to mark the Millennials:

1. Structured rule followers (Howe and Strauss, 2000; Zemke, Raines, and
   Filipczak, 2000)
2. Protected and sheltered (Howe and Strauss, 2000)
3. Confident and optimistic about their future (Martin and Tulgan, 2001;
   Schneider and Stevenson, 1999)
4. Conventionally motivated and respectful (Murray, 1997)
5. Cooperative and team-oriented (Howe and Strauss, 2000; Martin and
   Tulgan, 2001)
6. Pressured by and accepting of authority (Howe and Strauss, 2000;
   Murray, 1997)
7. Talented achievers (Lancaster and Stillman, 2002)

Given these impending characteristics, it is important to consider
how our understanding of the learning, growth, and development of these
students might be altered, and how a potentially new portrayal might
reshape the design and delivery of student services on college and university campuses.

Concerning the first point, these Millennial characteristics seem to call
into question some of the more commonly accepted assumptions about the
dynamics of development and maturation. For example, from a widely
applied model of identity development, articulated by Chickering and Reisser
(1993), comes an understanding of the role of interdependence, tolerance
for differences, and a sense of competence in the maturation of young adults.
Could it be that the Millennial emphasis on civic-mindedness, its more
diverse composition, and its achievement orientation will change the focus
of these issues in the lives of students? For example, personal autonomy and
independence have long been a prevailing attribute in most developmental
frameworks, extending from an assumption that, as individuals mature, they

must acquire a capacity to "do things on their own." Perhaps the Millennial civic-minded emphasis on cooperation and collaboration with others might further reorder the importance of independence in the scheme of human development, rendering it potentially a sign of regression and immaturity rather than positive growth. The revision of Chickering's seminal model (1969) to reflect a greater emphasis on interdependence over autonomy (Chickering and Reisser, 1993) seems to signal as much.

The sense of connectedness embedded in the Millennial experience, especially in a context of heightened cultural differences, might also raise standards of acceptance among members. Rather than *tolerance* of diversity (that is, passive acceptance) marking a milepost of maturity, perhaps successful *engagement* of (that is, interaction across) those differences will serve as a metric of even greater import along the path to young adulthood. As Dianna Eck (1993, p. 191) observed: "Diversity [in other words, *tolerance*] does not. . . . have to affect me. I can observe it. I can even celebrate diversity, as the cliché goes. But I have to participate in pluralism [that is, *engage differences*]. I can't just stand by and watch." Further, the realities of engagement in such a pluralistic world might entail that the practical will supplant the ideological in establishing effective policies and practices. What it takes to get something done (for example, negotiation and compromise), rather than faithfulness to principles and ideals, might become the more important measure of success.

From the perspective of cognitive development (for example, Baxter Magolda, 1992; King and Kitchener, 1994; Kohlberg, 1976; Perry, 1968), the Millennial generation's acquiescence to authority and social conventions might loom large in their developmental journey through intellectual and moral reasoning. For advancement to occur on most schemes of this nature, a form of personal autonomy and rejection of external authoritative bases of decision making are imminent. Could it be that the deference exhibited by such individuals might jeopardize or delay development in that regard? Will the unusual level of parental involvement in their lives attenuate their development of independent thinking? On the other hand, this generation of students comes to campus with a much greater exposure to moral relativism and the diversity of a politicized society. Perhaps these dynamics will, in fact, accelerate the kinds of contextual patterns that contribute to more advanced modes of thinking. Of course, it remains to be seen as this generation's dominant characteristics await full expression in our culture.

Finally, the heightened expectations for social aptitude and finesse that seem to accompany descriptions of these Millennials might also bear implications for their personal preferences, interests, and styles. If extraverts, social types, and assimilators (preferring reflective observation and abstract conceptualizing) seem to enjoy privileged positions in the socially oriented but analytically driven world of the academy, the future may hold a different promise with the advent of this new generation. Perhaps the extraverted social orientation will imbed itself further in the ethos of higher education and capitalize on the cooperative, team-oriented approach of these students. This, in turn, may shift the emphasis toward accommodation in learning (Kolb, 1983), where concrete experience and active experimentation emerge as the modes preferred over reflective observation and abstract conceptualizing. To be able to translate theory into practice may become as important as (if not more important than) understanding the theory itself, if these new students have their way.

The range of characteristics attributed to these rising Millennials might also cause us to question certain models and strategies we have come to rely on as student services practitioners. For example, their description as a watched-over, sheltered, and structured generation, with significant parental involvement, might challenge our expectations for their readiness to assume freedom, their savvy with regard to various safety risks, or their ability to manage their own time with productive activity. Perhaps these generational trends will entail a greater emphasis on structure and direction when designing, delivering, and even mandating student services, while assuming a greater role in teaching students how to relax, how to use free time, and how to translate the experience they already have in juggling many activities to their experience in higher education.

Furthermore, their sense of specialness and their being accustomed to focused individual attention, as well as having their needs and requests validated, may call for greater flexibility and problem solving on the part of practitioners. To be sure, the more highly educated and sophisticated Boomer parents of these students will not be far behind in terms of their expectations for the diligence, commitment, and excellence of all service providers on campus. If anything, standards will rise and demands will increase for promises to be met in reality. Of particular concern may be the need to be more patient with "fussy" parents "who will have more than the usual trouble letting go" (Howe and Strauss, 2000), assisting them with the transition they face in sending their daughters and sons to college and helping them promote their independence in a world where "breaking away" might prove the ultimate test.

The anticipated confident, optimistic, cooperative, and service orientation of these Millennials, as well as their abilities regarding leadership in support of change, suggest that we look carefully at our present inventory of campus opportunities for the engagement of these students. It will be ever more important to ensure an adequate balance of numbers of students and roles for significant involvement and achievement. This challenge calls for greater emphasis on human scale designs and systems in all dimensions of learning (Strange and Banning, 2001). More so, we may need to prepare to "run with" a new generation of students who are poised to make a difference in our institutions. However, even though they might be ready to become more involved, they may not know how to do so, independently, without a well-organized structure and defined authority.

Whatever the case might be, it seems clear that the Millennials, as currently understood, promise to reinvent some of the more commonly accepted constructions of growth and development during the college years, inasmuch as their valuing of community supplants individuality in their efforts to succeed. In such a context, perhaps "we connect" will replace "we differ" as the effective generational mantra, and a "community of the whole" (Spitzberg and Thorndike, 1992, p. 154)—in contrast to a "community of the parts"—will prevail on campus once again. In effect, the heritage of their civic prototype (Strauss and Howe, 1991) may position them to transform the naïve conformity of previous cohorts (for example, GI and Silent generations) to incorporate the political complexities of a diverse world whose survival depends on the reestablishment of stable institutions.

References

American College Personnel Association. *The Student Learning Imperative: Implications for Student Affairs.* Washington, D.C.: American College Personnel Association, 1994.

Atkinson, D., Morten, G., and Sue, D. *Counseling American Minorities: A Cross-Cultural Perspective* (2nd ed.). Dubuque, Iowa: Brown, 1983.

Baxter Magolda, M. *Knowing and Reasoning in College: Gender-Related Patterns in Students' Intellectual Development.* San Francisco: Jossey-Bass, 1992.

Baxter Magolda, M. *Creating Contexts for Learning and Self-Authorship: Constructive-Developmental Pedagogy.* Nashville, Tenn.: Vanderbilt University Press, 1999.

Cass, V. C. "Homosexual Identity Formation: A Theoretical Model." *Journal of Homosexuality,* 1979, *4,* 219–235.

Chickering, A. W. *Education and Identity.* San Francisco: Jossey-Bass, 1969.

Chickering, A., and Reisser, L. *Education and Identity* (2nd ed.). San Francisco: Jossey-Bass, 1993.

Cross, W. E., Jr. "The Psychology of Nigrescence: Revising the Cross Model." In J. G. Ponterotto, J. M. Casas, L. A. Suzuki, and C. M. Alexander (eds.), *Handbook of Multicultural Counseling.* Thousand Oaks, Calif.: Sage, 1995.

Eck, D. L. *Encountering God: A Spiritual Journey from Bozeman to Banaras.* Boston: Beacon Press, 1993.

Erikson, E. H. "Growth and Crisis of the Healthy Personality." In M.J.E. Senn (ed.), *Symposium on the Healthy Personality. Supplement II.* New York: Josiah Macy, Jr., Foundation, 1950.

Gilligan, C. *In a Different Voice: Psychological Theory and Women's Development.* Cambridge, Mass.: Harvard University Press, 1982.

Gitlin, T. *The Sixties: Years of Hope, Days of Rage.* New York: Bantam Books, 1987.

Holland, J. L. *Making Vocational Choices: A Theory of Careers.* Upper Saddle River, N.J.: Prentice Hall, 1973.

Howe, N., and Strauss, W. *Millennials Rising: The Next Great Generation.* New York: Vintage Books, 2000.

Josselson, R. *Finding Herself: Pathways to Identity Development in Women.* San Francisco: Jossey-Bass, 1987.

Keniston, K. "Social Change and Youth in America." In E. H. Erikson (ed.), *The Challenge of Youth.* New York: Doubleday, 1965.

King, P. M., and Kitchener, K. *Developing Reflective Judgment: Understanding and Promoting Intellectual Growth and Critical Thinking in Adolescents and Adults.* San Francisco: Jossey-Bass, 1994.

Kohlberg, L. "Moral Stages and Moralization: The Cognitive-Developmental Approach." In T. Lickona (ed.), *Moral Development and Behavior: Theory, Research, and Social Issues.* Austin, Tex.: Holt, Rinehart, and Winston, 1976.

Kolb, D. *Experiential Learning: Experience as the Source of Learning and Development.* Upper Saddle River, N.J.: Prentice Hall, 1983.

Kuh, G., and others. *Involving Colleges: Successful Approaches to Fostering Student Learning and Development Outside the Classroom.* San Francisco: Jossey-Bass, 1991.

Lancaster, L., and Stillman, D. *When Generations Collide: Who They Are. Why They Clash. How to Solve the Generational Puzzle at Work.* New York: HarperCollins, 2002.

Lasch, C. *The Culture of Narcissism: American Life in an Age of Diminishing Expectations.* New York: Norton, 1979.

Levine, A., and Cureton, J. S. *When Hope and Fear Collide: A Portrait of Today's College Student.* San Francisco: Jossey-Bass, 1998.

Levinson, D. J., and Associates. *Seasons of a Man's Life.* New York: Knopf, 1978.

Levinson, D. J., and Levinson, J. D. *The Seasons of a Woman's Life.* New York: Ballantine Books, 1996.

Martin, C. A., and Tulgan, B. *Managing Generation Y.* New Haven, Conn.: HRD Press, 2001.

Murray, N. D. "Welcome to the Future: The Millennial Generation." *Journal of Career Planning and Employment,* 1997, 57(3), 36–40.

Myers, I. B. *Gifts Differing.* Palo Alto, Calif.: Consulting Psychologists Press, 1980.

Neugarten, B. L. "Adult Personality: Toward a Psychology of the Life Cycle." In B. L. Neugarten (ed.), *Middle Age and Aging.* Chicago: University of Chicago Press, 1968.

Newton, F. B. "The New Student." *About Campus,* 2000, 5(5), 8–15.

Perry, W. *Forms of Intellectual and Ethical Development in the College Years: A Scheme.* Austin, Tex.: Holt, Rinehart, and Winston, 1968.

Schneider, B., and Stevenson, D. *The Ambitious Generation: America's Teenagers, Motivated But Directionless.* New Haven, Conn.: Yale University Press, 1999.

Spitzberg Jr., I. J., and Thorndike, V. V. *Creating Community on College Campuses.* Albany: State University of New York Press, 1992.

Strange, C. "Student Development: The Evolution and Status of an Essential Idea." *Journal of College Student Development,* 1994, 39, 87–99.

Strange, C., and Banning, J. *Educating by Design: Creating Campus Learning Environments That Work.* San Francisco: Jossey-Bass, 2001.

Strauss, W., and Howe, N. *Generations: The History of America's Future, 1584 to 2069.* New York: Morrow, 1991.

Zemke, R., Raines, C., and Filpczak, R. *Generations at Work: Managing the Clash of Veterans, Boomers, Xers, and Nexters in Your Workplace.* New York: AMACOM, 2000.

C. CARNEY STRANGE is professor of higher education and student affairs at Bowling Green State University in Ohio.

Literature on teaching and learning in college classrooms is reviewed and findings are discussed through a generational lens. From assumptions about generations of students, recommendations for enhancing student learning—especially for Millennial students—are provided.

5

Teaching, Learning, and Millennial Students

Maureen E. Wilson

A growing body of literature has focused on improving undergraduate education and teaching. In classrooms and beyond, educators can create environments and experiences to enhance student learning and engagement. Among the many recommendations for improving teaching and learning, Barr and Tagg (1995) encouraged a paradigm shift from emphasizing teaching to emphasizing learning. In the learning paradigm, the mission and purpose of education is to produce learning, not to deliver instruction. Rather than faculty being primarily lecturers, they are designers of learning methods and environments. This shift is consistent with the principles that are described next.

On the basis of fifty years of research on teaching, Chickering and Gamson (1987) published *Seven Principles for Good Practice in Undergraduate Education.* These good practices (1) encourage contact between students and faculty, (2) develop reciprocity and cooperation among students, (3) encourage active learning, (4) give prompt feedback, (5) emphasize time on task, (6) communicate high expectations, and (7) respect diverse talents and ways of knowing. These principles, in combination with other research, can help those interested in enhancing teaching effectiveness with the Millennial generation.

Elements of Effective Teaching

Using Chickering and Gamson's principles as a framework, I examine strategies for teaching in light of Millennial student characteristics.

NEW DIRECTIONS FOR STUDENT SERVICES, no. 106, Summer 2004 © Wiley Periodicals, Inc.

Student-Faculty Contact. Many scholars emphasize the importance of student-faculty contact in higher education (Braxton, Eimers, and Bayer, 1996; Chickering and Gamson, 1987; Guskin, 1994; King, 2003). Frequent student-faculty contact can enhance students' motivation, involvement, and intellectual commitment, encouraging them to think about their own values and future plans (Chickering and Gamson, 1987). However, it is the quality of the contact, not the quantity, that matters (Cross, 1999; Kuh, 2003). Cross (1999) suggested that more successful students may be more likely than less successful students to seek contact with faculty and reap the benefits, and that perhaps "faculty who invite frequent student contacts are more likely to be the kind of people who stimulate educational satisfaction than faculty who are not so easily approachable" (p. 264). She argued that we know, from a combination of research and experience, that "when faculty show an interest in students, get to know them through informal as well as formal channels, engage in conversations with them, [and] show interest in their intellectual development, then students respond with enthusiasm and engagement" (p. 264).

According to Kuh (2003), "student-faculty interaction matters most to learning when it encourages students to devote greater effort to other educationally purposeful activities during college" (p. 29). Substantive contact between students and faculty is what matters, and most goals do not require extensive contact. For instance, discussing career plans with faculty or working with them on a project or committee outside of class could happen just once or twice a year. Joining a professor on a research project once during college could have a major impact on a student. Other activities need to happen much more frequently: receiving prompt feedback, discussing course requirements and grades, and discussing ideas outside of class (Kuh, 2003).

One important step in building relationships with students is to know them by name and seek informal contact with them. Because only 35.6 percent of entering first-year students estimated chances were very good that they would communicate regularly with professors (Sax and others, 2002), faculty may need to take the lead in establishing norms that facilitate connections with students. Those Millennials who had a sheltered upbringing and parents who advocated for them will need to learn how to deal with authorities and advocate for themselves.

Reciprocity and Cooperation. Chickering and Gamson (1987) argued that working with others can increase involvement in learning and that discussion can improve thinking and deepen understanding. Described as team-oriented (Howe and Strauss, 2003), many Millennials grew up working in groups and playing on teams. Might they consequently face difficulties in learning to think independently and articulate their positions? Although anecdotal reports indicate that students prepare less for classes using group work and rely on peers to help them, Kuh (2003) suggested that this phenomenon can be minimized by incorporating peer evaluation, grading individual contributions to group projects, and observing group activities.

One aspect of reciprocity and cooperation is to consider a class as a group and address the dynamics therein. Teaching and learning are influenced by a variety of social factors, including social status (gender, race, age, and social class of students and instructors), role relationships (interaction patterns between and among faculty and students that affect who participates and how), and structural inequalities (power differences between faculty and students and how faculty use or share their authority; Hirschy and Wilson, 2002). Cooperation among students can be promoted by focusing on the social dynamics in a class. Hirschy and Wilson argued that "by anticipating and attending to the social forces that occur in the classroom, faculty better foster student learning and help students achieve their higher education goals" (p. 97).

Fassinger (1995) argued that course design can have the greatest impact of all on class participation. Faculty can cultivate interaction when they create class activities such as study groups and learning partners that foster the positive emotional climate developed when students are "cooperative and supportive and make friends in class" (p. 94). Findings from her research suggested that efforts to develop the students' confidence are likely to promote participation in class. Students fear appearing unintelligent to their peers and professors, thus hampering participation. Therefore, promoting norms for classroom interaction and having discussion that helps to develop empathy for classmates can increase involvement; "facilitating students' willingness to raise questions or offer comments in class is likely to enhance their intellectual development" (Fassinger, 1995, p. 82).

Millennial students are described as cooperative team players (Howe and Strauss, 2000). They have likely experienced more cooperative and collaborative learning environments prior to college. This could bode well for their willingness and ability to work with peers in college classrooms to enhance learning.

Active Learning. Cooperative and collaborative learning are two forms of active learning, another of the seven principles. McKeachie (2002) argued that "discussion methods are superior to lectures in student retention of information after the end of a course; transfer of knowledge to new situations; development of problem solving, thinking, or attitude change; and motivation for further learning" (pp. 52–53). In contrast to listening to lectures, memorizing information, and repeating it on exams, students reap greater benefits when they engage with material, relate it to their experiences, and apply it to their lives (Chickering and Gamson, 1987). Guskin (1994) argued that the passive lecture-discussion format so common for undergraduate students is contrary to most principles for promoting optimal student learning.

To promote learning, students need to be engaged and involved. Cress and Sax (1998) cited research indicating that an increasing number of faculty are using student-centered pedagogy and active learning strategies. Fewer lectures and more discussions, cooperative learning, and group projects are examples of more engaging approaches to teaching; "active learners tend to be more tolerant of new ideas, are able to develop multiple ways [of] solving problems, work collaboratively with other students, and are self-motivated" (Cress and Sax, 1998, p. 76). The team orientation of Millennials ought to work well with active learning strategies, among them cooperative and collaborative learning.

Feedback. Most reports on enhancing undergraduate education emphasize the importance of frequent, prompt, and constructive feedback to students (Braxton, Eimers, and Bayer, 1996). Chickering and Gamson (1987) stressed that students need opportunities to reflect on their learning and how to assess themselves.

In arguing that "how individuals construct knowledge and use their knowledge is closely tied to their sense of self," King and Baxter Magolda (1991) wrote that students' ability to hear and respond to suggestions and criticisms depends on their cognitive complexity and emotional maturity. Therefore, educators must provide feedback according to the needs and abilities of a particular student and "understand the role of support in the developmental process" (p. 602).

All students can benefit from timely feedback, delivered effectively, to help them learn. More frequent quizzes and smaller assignments can provide feedback to students *and* faculty and reduce the pressure of succeeding or failing on the basis of a few heavily weighted examinations. It also creates a greater variety of formats that can play to the different strengths of students and encourage others to develop new academic skills. This feedback can also assist students who are striving to meet high expectations and may also increase their time on task—two more of the seven principles.

Time on Task. Another principle of good practice emphasizes time on task. Highly involved and scheduled, Millennial students have been shuttled to activities and lessons with very little free time and may continue to join numerous clubs and organizations on campus. Students must devote adequate time and effort to educationally purposeful activity to enhance learning (King, 2003). One measure of this is the amount of time students devote to studying. Students expect to study more often in college than high school, and they do. Their time doubles in college to about twelve hours per week, but this means that most students are only spending about half of the commonly recommended study time of two hours outside of class for every hour in class (Kuh, 2003).

It appears that Millennial students experience academic success in high school with relatively little effort (Sax, 2003). In the Higher Education Research Institute's annual survey of first year students, 45.7 percent reported average high school grades of A+, A, or A− and 49 percent reported a B+, B, or B− average. More reported A+ or A than B. Most respondents (60.2 percent) "believe there is a 'very good chance' that they will earn at least a B average in college" (Sax, 2003, p. 17). Most studied little during their senior year; 37.9 percent spent two hours or less, 28.6 percent spent three to five hours, and 33.4 percent spent six or more (Sax and others, 2002).

Kuh (2003) said there is no substitute for time on task: "[Time on task] is even more important if we think of engagement as a valued end in itself. College is a potentially transforming experience, a once-in-a-lifetime opportunity to challenge students to examine their previous ways of knowing, thinking, and behaving. It's hard to imagine this happening to a meaningful degree if students don't devote the time and effort needed to develop the habits of the mind and heart characteristic of an educated person" (p. 28).

Although Millennials are described as confident and achieving (Howe and Strauss, 2003), there is a disconnect between aspirations and efforts. Therefore, one goal of educators should be to assist students in developing realistic expectations of the amount and quality of effort required to be academically successful, especially if they want to meet another goal of graduate school. Nearly three-quarters of participants in the 2002 Higher Education Research Institute study reported planning to pursue a graduate degree, including 17.4 percent desiring a Ph.D. or Ed.D.

High Expectations. When teachers and institutions expect students to perform well, it becomes a self-fulfilling prophecy for students, who are likely to exert more effort to meet expectations (Chickering and Gamson, 1987; Kuh, 2003). Conversely, low expectations are usually met with low effort and performance. Millennials who were closely monitored, sheltered, and pushed to excel have faced academic pressure via testing and accountability procedures promulgated by Baby Boomers. Having been "taught to the test," students need to learn to think critically and with more complexity than some of them have done in the past.

Kuh posited that "students will go beyond what they think they can do under certain conditions, one of which is that their teachers expect, challenge, and support them to do so. Students read and write when we demand it" (p. 28). The work required to meet high expectations combined with prompt feedback and other effective teaching practices results in more learning.

However, high expectations require more time from everyone, violating the "disengagement compact" (p. 28)—a bargain struck between professors and students to leave each other alone. Instead, students must work harder to prepare for class and complete assignments, while faculty must devote significant time to grading assignments, providing feedback, and meeting with students to discuss assignments and feedback. Given typical faculty reward structures, especially at research universities, time devoted to teaching competes with other priorities, including research. According to Astin, Keup, and Lindholm (2002), independent liberal arts colleges have shown a larger increase in faculty-student interaction than public and private universities, and this gap has widened during the past decade. Kuh believes there is "a breakdown of shared responsibility for learning" where faculty do not expect students' maximal effort and students do not take full advantage of institutional resources (Kuh, 2003, p. 28).

Some signs indicate that students think highly of their abilities and are striving to meet high expectations. According to the annual study of first-year students (Sax and others, 2002), a majority of respondents ranked themselves above average or in the highest 10 percent in academic ability (69.5 percent) and in intellectual self-confidence (60.1 percent). Interestingly, a minority of respondents ranked their writing (46.4 percent) and mathematics (45.2 percent) ability as above average or in the highest 10 percent. Furthermore, 59.7 percent of students reported taking advanced placement courses in high school, and 46.4 percent took advanced placement exams. In 2002, the average SAT math score reached a thirty-two-year high of 516, up 15 points from 1992. Females hit a thirty-five-year high of 500, while the male average was 534. Of female college-bound seniors, 44 percent took precalculus, a rise of 13 percent in ten years. Unfortunately, the average verbal score declined in 2002 and is just four points higher than in 1992. Gaston Caperton, president of the College Board, says that the math scores are the result of efforts to improve math education in the United States. "It is time to put that same kind of concerted energy behind ensuring that students reach their potential as skilled readers and writers," he said (College Board, 2002, sect. 4). Improving the writing abilities of students requires great effort from students and faculty. It also requires high expectations of faculty and students to be successful.

Diverse Talents and Ways of Knowing. Good practice in undergraduate education also respects diverse talents and ways of learning (Chickering and Gamson, 1987). Because students' talents and learning styles differ, teachers should use a variety of teaching and assessment strategies. Although many assume that learning styles are correlated to race, ethnicity, gender, and culture, King (2003) suggests that this assumption may be premature and based on limited research with college students. She wrote, "Students of all cultural and racial backgrounds should be encouraged to develop learning strategies that are flexible and suited for the specific demands and constraints of the problem at hand" (p. 255). Therefore, teachers who employ active learning techniques, help students develop a variety of strategies for learning, and assist them in determining which ones are likely to be most effective in a particular situation are able to enhance educational outcomes for students.

Teaching Millennials

As explained in greater depth elsewhere in this volume, students from the Millennial generation who began arriving on college campuses around 2000 are described as special, sheltered, confident, team-oriented, conventional, pressured, achieving, optimistic and upbeat, accepting of authority, rule followers, and structured. They had closely supervised upbringings and are smarter than most think, technologically savvy, and becoming more politically conservative, while holding more liberal attitudes toward social issues (Howe and Strauss, 2000, 2003; Rooney, 2003). Howe and Strauss (2003) claimed that Millennials on campus will be close with their parents, very focused on grades and performance, busy in extracurricular activities, eager for community activities, talented in technology, more interested in math and science, less interested in the humanities, demanding of a secure and regulated environment, respectful of norms and institutions, conventionally minded, conformist in thinking, ethnically diverse, and majority female (p. 32). Murray (1997) claims Millennials are more trusting of systems, bred for success, willing to work hard, comfortable with groups, and not very self-reflective; "they will expect us to display authoritative expertise, model effective techniques, stress motivation, invest in their outcomes, celebrate their victories" (p. 42). In light of these characteristics and the principles for effective teaching already addressed here, this section presents recommendations for continuing to enhance opportunities for teaching and learning for Millennial students.

High Expectations. Millennials are likely to invest themselves to meet high and clear expectations. Murray (1997) suggested that Millennial students are "better prepared, more confident, and. . . . more willing to do what it takes to succeed" (p. 42) than the Generation X students who preceded them. Because they were raised to devote much time and energy to achieving goals and have been rewarded for doing so, he believes they will continue to do so in college. Given how structured their lives have been, they may struggle in the transition to college as they face more ambiguity and a greater call for self-responsibility. They are likely to appreciate clear expectations, explicit syllabi, and well-structured assignments, for example. Desiring to achieve, many will expect detailed instructions and guidelines for completing assignments and knowing what will be covered on tests. What exactly must be done to earn an A? For educators, this presents challenges since learning, growth, and development require increasingly complex thinking, greater autonomy and reliance on self, and less reliance on authorities. Reliant, cooperative, and compliant Millennials who largely share their parents' values may be less likely to challenge authority and the status quo. To the chagrin of many, they should be encouraged to do so.

Furthermore, Millennial students who have achieved academic success with relatively little effort may have unrealistic expectations about what is necessary to be academically successful in college (Sax, 2003). Sax suggested that high-achieving students may become demoralized by earning a B or C in college. Therefore, students may require help to improve their study and time management skills and encouragement to meet with faculty. Faculty can "[create] study groups and other forms of collaborative learning" (pp. 19–20) to assist students in meeting high expectations.

Parental Involvement. Many scholars expect an unprecedented level of parental involvement with Millennial students and their colleges. Jacobson (2003) described parents who have been actively involved in their students' lives, not just delivering their children to activities and events but staying there to cheer for them. It seems unlikely they will suddenly step back now. Howe and Strauss (2003) argued that Millennials have been sheltered. The Baby Boomer parents who put "baby on board" signs in their car windows have also promoted tougher policies for school security, drug enforcement, driver's licenses, music labeling (for explicit lyrics), and television (warnings for content).

On campus, admissions officials suspect that ever more applications are completed by parents, and some parents threaten lawsuits when admission is denied (Jacobson, 2003). Although some students appear embarrassed when parents grill campus administrators, many expect their parents to play an active role in their college search and experience. Instead of dropping students off at the college residence hall, parents are often invited by colleges to stay for parents' orientation; some institutions have developed an office for parental relations. Beyond the classroom, parents' involvement with students is promoted through parental notification policies to inform parents of a student's drug or alcohol violation. Regarding academics, actively involved parents—or intrusive ones—may be more likely to be actively involved in choosing courses and majors for students, to contact professors about grades, attend hearings for academic dishonesty, and monitor course content, particularly as it relates to controversial issues. Exposure to differing points of view can help students articulate their values and positions on difficult and complex issues, especially when challenged to do so by faculty and administrators.

As Baby Boomer parents have fought successfully for changes in the Family Educational Rights and Privacy Act to allow notification on some student conduct issues, might they also work for greater sharing of academic information? Might more parents begin to contact faculty to monitor student progress? Will it be necessary if students willingly share this information with parents whom they view as personal supports and advocates?

Technology. Students are increasingly savvy when it comes to technology, though not all students will be proficient. Cress and Sax (1998) warned that colleges should address "technologically disadvantaged" (p. 77) students, often first-generation and from working-class families. These students may have less experience with and access to the technologies that many take for granted. Increasing reliance on technology has several implications for teaching. First, most students will expect faculty to incorporate technology into their teaching and to be proficient in using it. At a minimum, communication with faculty via e-mail and access to online resources will be expected. Other technologies such as PowerPoint presentations, Internet activities, online discussions, and electronic classrooms may be available as well. Howe and Strauss (2003) predicted that Millennials will want to learn how to apply technology to fix social problems such as global warming. However, Grasha and Yangarber-Hicks (2000) emphasize the importance for faculty to develop a conceptual rationale for incorporating technology into their teaching, identifying how it fits with their philosophy of teaching and learning. In other words, technology should not be used for its own sake but rather only if it enhances teaching and learning.

Some campuses have been successful in enhancing student learning through a combination of pedagogical and technological innovations (Twigg, 2002). For example, online quizzes can provide immediate feedback (one of the seven principles) and direct students to material so as to review and improve understanding. Web-based homework that is graded automatically can increase time on task (another principle) by presenting more problems to solve than can be reasonably graded by hand.

As most students will be comfortable with the Internet, they will naturally use it as an academic resource. Faculty, then, must help students evaluate the credibility of those sources (Canada, 2000). The University of Michigan (Irwin, 2003), for instance, has a resource for students to help them learn how to evaluate Web sites. Through a series of questions, students are guided to determine the intention (author's motivation, point of view expressed, quality and accuracy of content, completeness of coverage), relevance (currency of information), and reliability (authority and authorship) of a site. Using examples from the Internet, faculty could tailor this activity to a particular course, discussing in class the intention, relevance, and reliability of selected sites.

Issues of academic honesty and intellectual ownership also flow from this reliance on the Internet: "The ease of going online has shaped not only attitudes about downloading, but cheating as well, blurring the lines between right and wrong. . . . Students generally know not to buy a paper off the Internet, but many think it is OK to pull a paragraph or two, as long as they change a few words" (Zernike, 2003, p. A6).

Perhaps related to real and perceived pressure to excel, some students are willing to cheat to succeed. Although most students know that quoting sources word-for-word requires a citation, some believe that paraphrasing does not (McCabe, Trevino, and Butterfield, 2001). Furthermore, in a study of academic dishonesty among high school students, McCabe (1999) reported that they felt their teachers were unfamiliar with the Internet and that it was easy to download papers to plagiarize assignments. Those students may continue that perception as college students. To discourage cheating in all forms, faculty should discuss these issues with students, first to promote an environment of academic integrity and second to communicate clear expectations for appropriate academic standards. If it is true that Millennial students are rule followers (Howe and Strauss, 2000), they must first know the rules if they are to follow them. Conversely, Newton (2000) suggested that although students know the rules, they also know how to circumvent them and embrace a "cheating is OK if you do not get caught" philosophy (p. 12). Although Millennials are not the first generation to cheat and they will not be the last, the fact that many more high-tech opportunities exist to facilitate academic dishonesty creates new challenges for dealing effectively with it.

In a related issue, increasing reliance on electronic resources may make getting students to actually walk into the campus library increasingly difficult. The explosion of online databases along with access to full-text articles makes it tempting to use only resources accessible via computer. As a graduate faculty member, I have seen bright students ignore timely, relevant, and important resources because the full text was not available online or they lacked access to it in that format. One student claimed the library did not own a major journal in her field of study, unaware that bound journals were on the shelves. Informed of this, she was reluctant to go locate and photocopy articles from it.

Another issue related to technology is that an increasing number of students may enroll in online courses that, by design, rely heavily on technology. Indeed, one campus has instituted a requirement that all students take at least one online course each year; others offer hybrid or blended courses—a mix of traditional and virtual classrooms (Young, 2002). Knowlton (2000) argued that online courses should reflect a student-centered paradigm, not a professor-centered one. In contrast to a lecture during which students take notes, a professor in a student-centered classroom "serves as a facilitator while students collaborate with each other and the professor to develop personal understanding of content" (p. 7). The teacher's role, then, "is to *frame* the course and supplement student interactions by providing resources and opportunities" (p. 11). By actively involving students, this approach is consistent with Chickering and Gamson's principles (1987).

Finally, both faculty and students influence the classroom environment; peers have a strong effect on student learning (Hirschy and Wilson, 2002). Therefore, teachers should know about the influence of technology on their relationships with students and among students. Nowhere is the issue more obvious than in online courses, where developing relationships with and among students is especially challenging sans face-to-face contact. Canada (2000) and Weiss (2000) offer suggestions for developing connections in online courses, among them posting brief biographies, scheduling group activities such as a trip to the library, creating a virtual break room for chats, and adding written cues in communications through words or symbols to indicate tone.

Students with Disabilities. From 1978 to 1998, the percentage of first-year college students with a disability tripled from 3 percent to 9 percent, and the number continues to grow (National Council on Disability, 2003). Estimates of the number of college students with attention deficit hyperactivity disorder—just one of many learning disabilities—range from 65,000 to 650,000 (Farrell, 2003). A substantial number of students are not diagnosed with a learning disability until college (National Council on

Disability, 2003). Those Millennial students who were diagnosed as children likely had individual education plans in primary and secondary school. They may have received medication at home and school to control their symptoms and academic accommodations such as separate rooms for testing or additional time on tests and assignments. A professional at the National Center for Learning Disabilities said it is crucial for college students to self-advocate and talk with professors about their disability and what assistance they need. This may be new behavior as parents worked with school officials to coordinate those services in high school (Farrell, 2003). Furthermore, faculty need to be educated to work effectively with students with disabilities.

As Farrell (2003) describes, students with learning disabilities face multiple challenges in the move from high school to college. A noisy residence hall and little supervision can replace a quiet home supervised by parents. Lengthy class periods in college can interfere with a short attention span. Variable class scheduling can disrupt routine. Course grades can be determined with a few assignments instead of multiple, shorter assignments that are checked regularly. Parents who keep a close eye on students and are in regular contact with teachers are unlikely to have that access to college professors. As college students must take increasing responsibility for coping with their disabilities (both physical and learning), faculty and student affairs administrators are advised to assist students in the transition as they learn what it will take to succeed in college and beyond.

Every generation of students brings its own history, strengths, and challenges to campus; general group characteristics do not describe accurately or well any individual student. Still, faculty and administrators can anticipate many of the issues likely to affect Millennial students and develop strategies for working effectively with them. Combined with a passion for teaching, the recommendations included here can assist educators in engaging with a new generation of students to promote critical thinking, active engagement, and lifelong learning.

References

Astin, A. W., Keup, J. R., and Lindholm, J. A. "A Decade of Changes in Undergraduate Education: A National Study of System 'Transformation.'" *Review of Higher Education,* 2002, 25(2), 141–162.

Barr, R. B., and Tagg, J. "From Teaching to Learning: A New Paradigm for Undergraduate Education." *Change,* 1995, 27(6), 12–25.

Braxton, J. M., Eimers, M. T., and Bayer, A. E. "The Implications of Teaching Norms for the Improvement of Undergraduate Education." *Journal of Higher Education,* 1996, 67(6), 603–625.

Canada, M. "Students as Seekers in Online Courses." In R. E. Weiss, D. S. Knowlton, and B. W. Speck (eds.), *Principles of Effective Teaching in the Online Classroom.* New Directions for Teaching and Learning, no. 84. San Francisco: Jossey-Bass, 2000.

Chickering, A. W., and Gamson, Z. F. "Seven Principles for Good Practice in Undergraduate Education." *AAHE Bulletin,* 1987, 39(7), 3–7.

College Board. "10-Year Trend in SAT Scores Indicates Increased Emphasis on Math Is Yielding Results; Reading and Writing Are Causes for Concern." Aug. 27, 2002. Retrieved Apr. 26, 2004, from http://www.collegeboard.com/press/article/0,1433,11752,%2000.html.

Cress, C. M., and Sax, L. J. "Campus Climate Issues to Consider for the Next Decade." In K. W. Bauer (ed.), *Campus Climate: Understanding the Critical Components of Today's Colleges and Universities.* New Directions for Institutional Research, no. 98. San Francisco: Jossey-Bass, 1998.

Cross, K. P. "What Do We Know About Students' Learning, and How Do We Know It?" *Innovative Higher Education,* 1999, 23(4), 255–270.

Farrell, E. F. "Paying Attention to Students Who Can't." *Chronicle of Higher Education,* Sept. 26, 2003, p. A50.

Fassinger, P. A. "Understanding Classroom Interaction: Students' and Professors' Contributions to Students' Silence." *Journal of Higher Education,* 1995, 66(1), 82–96.

Grasha, A. F., and Yangarber-Hicks, N. "Integrating Teaching Styles and Learning Styles with Instructional Technology." *College Teaching,* 2000, 48(1), 2–10.

Guskin, A. E. "Restructuring the Role of Faculty." *Change,* 1994, 26(5), 16–25.

Hirschy, A. S., and Wilson, M. E. "The Sociology of the Classroom and Its Influence on Student Learning." *Peabody Journal of Education,* 2002, 77(3), 85–100.

Howe, N., and Strauss, W. *Millennials Rising: The Next Great Generation.* New York: Vintage Books, 2000.

Howe, N., and Strauss, W. *Millennials Go to College.* Great Falls, Va.: American Association of Registrars and Admissions Officers and LifeCourse Associates, 2003.

Irwin, K. "Criteria for Web Site Evaluation." Ann Arbor, Mich.: Regents of the University of Michigan, 2003. Retrieved Apr. 26, 2004, from http://www.lib.umich.edu/ugl/guides/evaluation/main.html.

Jacobson, J. "Help Not Wanted." *Chronicle of Higher Education,* July 18, 2003, pp. A27–A28.

King, P. M. "Student Learning in Higher Education." In S. R. Komives, D. B. Woodard, and Associates, *Student Services: A Handbook for the Profession* (4th ed.). San Francisco: Jossey-Bass, 2003.

King P. M., and Baxter Magolda, M. B. "A Developmental Perspective on Learning." *Journal of College Student Development,* 1991, 40(5), 599–609.

Knowlton, D. S. "A Theoretical Framework for the Online Classroom: A Defense and Delineation of a Student-Centered Pedagogy." In R. E. Weiss, D. S. Knowlton, and B. W. Speck (eds.), *Principles of Effective Teaching in the Online Classroom.* New Directions for Teaching and Learning, no. 84. San Francisco: Jossey-Bass, 2000.

Kuh, G. D. "What We're Learning About Student Engagement from NSSE." *Change,* 2003, 35(2), 24–32.

McCabe, D. L. "Academic Dishonesty Among High School Students." *Adolescence,* 1999, 34(136), 681–687.

McCabe, D. L., Trevino, L. K., and Butterfield, K. D. "Cheating in Academic Institutions: A Decade of Research." *Ethics and Behavior,* 2001, 11(3), 219–232.

McKeachie, W. J. *Teaching Tips: Strategies, Research and Theory for College and University Teachers* (11th ed.). Boston: Houghton Mifflin, 2002.

Murray, N. D. "Welcome to the Future: The Millennial Generation." *Journal of Career Planning and Employment,* 1997, 57(3), 36–40.

National Council on Disability. "People with Disabilities and Postsecondary Education." Sept. 15, 2003. Retrieved April 26, 2004, from http://www.ncd.gov/newsroom/publications/2003/education.htm.

Newton, F. B. "The New Student." *About Campus,* 2000, 5(5), 8–15.

Rooney, M. "Freshmen Show Rising Political Awareness and Changing Social Views." *Chronicle of Higher Education,* Jan. 31, 2003, p. A35–38.

Sax, L. J. "Our Incoming Students: What Are They Like?" *About Campus,* 2003, 8(3), 15–20.

Sax, L. J., Lindholm, J. A., Astin, A. W., Korn, W. S., and Mahoney, K. M. *The American Freshman: National Norms for Fall 2002.* Los Angeles: Higher Education Research Institute, 2002.

Twigg, C. A. "Rethinking the Seven Principles." *Learning Marketspace,* Nov. 1, 2002. Retrieved Apr. 26, 2004, from http://www.center.rpi.edu/lforum/lm/nov02.html.

Weiss, R. E. "Humanizing the Online Classroom." In R. E. Weiss, D. S. Knowlton, and B. W. Speck (eds.), *Principles of Effective Teaching in the Online Classroom.* New Directions for Teaching and Learning, no. 84. San Francisco: Jossey-Bass, 2000.

Young, J. R. "'Hybrid' Teaching Seeks to End the Divide Between Traditional and Online Instruction." *Chronicle of Higher Education,* Mar. 22, 2002, p. A33.

Zernike, K. "Students Shall Not Download. Yeah, Sure." *New York Times,* Sept. 20. 2003, p. A6.

MAUREEN E. WILSON is assistant professor of higher education and student affairs at Bowling Green State University in Ohio.

6

The Millennial generation of college students has demographics and attitudes toward diversity issues different from their predecessors; this chapter explores those differences and their implications for student affairs work.

Understanding Diversity in Millennial Students

Ellen M. Broido

College students of the new millennium are different from their predecessors in many ways, among them having distinct demographic characteristics, views of people different from themselves, political and social values, and attitudes about social justice issues. As the Millennial generation brings these differences with them to college, university administrators need to rethink how they attempt to address social justice and diversity issues on campus.

Changing Student Demographics

One highly visible way in which Millennial students differ from earlier students is their racial and ethnic diversity. According to the 2000 U.S. census, 39.1 percent of people under eighteen are people of color (Asian; black; Hispanic, who may be of any race; or Native American), as compared to 28.02 percent of people eighteen and over (U.S. Census Bureau, 2001a, 2002). The growing percentage of young people of color is likely to be reflected in the student population. According to the Educational Testing Service (Carnevale and Fry, 2000), "The increase in African American undergraduates will be relatively modest—from 12.8 percent of students in 1995 to 13.2 percent in 2015. Asians on campus will swell dramatically by 86 percent over the 1995 level, growing from 5.4 percent of college students to 8.4 percent. Hispanic students, too, will register large increases, from 10.6 percent of 1995 undergraduates to 15.4 percent in 2015. . . . Minority enrollment will rise both in absolute numbers of students—up about 2 million—and in percentage terms, up from 29.4 percent of undergraduate enrollment to 37.2 percent" (p. 9).

Millennial students also are far more likely to be biracial or multiracial than are previous generations. This group made up 3.95 percent of the under-eighteen population in the 2000 U.S. census, while they made up just 0.95 percent of the eighteen-and-over population. Moreover, the fraction of biracial and multiracial children in the population grows in each successively younger age group; this group makes up only 3.15 percent of those fourteen to seventeen years old in 2000 while they were 5.35 percent of those who were less than one year old in 2000. Biracial and multiracial students are most likely to be most visible at institutions that draw their students from urban areas, especially in the southwestern United States, and the East and West Coasts (Rosenblatt, 1999). At these institutions the "check one box" racial categories on university forms make little sense to an increasing fraction of the student body (Renn, 1998). Moreover, informal reports indicate that an increasing number of college students are refusing to identify their race at all.

The rise in the number of people of color does not necessarily translate into increased intergroup contact, particularly between whites and people of color, because neighborhoods and schools tend to be racially segregated. According to research done under the auspices of the Lewis Mumford Center for Comparative and Urban Research (Logan and others, 2001), "children of all groups are being raised in environments where their own groups' size is inflated, and where they are under-exposed to children of other racial and ethnic backgrounds" (p. 1). However, this reality is shifting, slowly for white children's contact with children of color, much more rapidly for contact between racial or ethnic minority children. Between 1990 and 2000, there was a greater than 10 percent decrease in the level of segregation between black children and Asian and Hispanic children (Logan and others, 2001). White children in metropolitan areas are living in somewhat more racially mixed neighborhoods than they did a decade ago; however, racial and ethnic minority "children have lower exposure to white children in their neighborhoods now than was true ten years ago" (p. 4).

Simultaneously, after decades of progress toward desegregation of children's schools, that change generally has halted, and in some places, particularly in metropolitan areas, schools are becoming more segregated than they were a decade ago (Logan, 2002). Currently, "at the national level. . . white, black, and Hispanic elementary children on average all attend schools where their group is a majority" (p. 3). Thus, although campuses generally will become increasingly diverse, interracial contact is likely to be a new experience for many (especially white) college students.

However, this will not be the experience at all campuses. Because of the urbanization of people of color (whites are about twice as likely to live in rural areas as are Asians, blacks, or Hispanics; Battelle, 2000), rural campuses that draw their students from local regions may remain over-whelmingly white institutions.

One reason the Millennial generation has a racial and ethnic profile different from that of earlier generations is the rising number of immigrants to the United States. According to Howe and Strauss (2000), 20 percent of this generation have at least one parent who is an immigrant. According to the U.S. Census Bureau (2001b), half of those living in the United States who are foreign-born are from Latin America, and a quarter are from Asia. This immigrant population is highly concentrated in urban areas and along the East and West Coasts of the United States (as well as a few very large mid-western cities).

Not surprisingly, given the increasing number of children who are immigrants or children of immigrants, the Millennial generation reflects a different level of English language proficiency than do recent generations (a century ago, immigrants made up a slightly larger fraction of the U.S. population than they do currently, although immigration rates were appreciably lower in the intervening years; Camerota, 2002). The total number of children and young adult students who speak languages other than English at home has roughly doubled since 1979. According to Livingston and Wirt (2003), in 1999 17 percent of five-to-twenty-four-year-olds spoke a language other than English at home. Although speaking a language other than English at home is by no means a guarantee that a person does not speak English well, 6 percent of the participants in Livingston and Wirt's study were identified as able to speak English less than very well.

Race, ethnicity, immigration status, and English language skills are not the only ways in which the Millennial generation differs from earlier ones. The distribution of wealth has become more polarized in the United States over the last fifteen years, according to Pear (2002), who drew upon 2002 census data. The Center on Budget and Policy Priorities (2003) reiterated this point, writing that "after-tax income was more heavily concentrated at the top of the income scale than at any other time in the 1979–2000 period" (p. 1).

This shift in income is relevant for understanding Millennial college students because access to college is restricted for students from less wealthy families. According to Burd (2001), "the gap in the college-going rates between students from low-income families and those from high-income families is nearly as wide as it was three decades ago" (p. A26). A 2001 report of the Advisory Committee on Student Financial Assistance, a group that advises Congress on student financial aid policy, stated that "low-income students, who are at least minimally qualified or better, attend four-year institutions at half the rate of their comparably qualified high-income peers" (p. v). This problem has been exacerbated by shifts in private and state-based financial aid awards from need to merit and from grants to loans, and the decreasing purchasing power of Pell Grants.

Additional demographic shifts will be evident in the Millennial generation. People can become aware of their sexual orientation at any point in their lives, but data indicate that an increasing number of students are coming out as lesbian, gay, and bisexual, even as early as elementary school (Cahill, Ellen, and Tobias, 2003; Human Rights Watch, 2001). Because of the stigma of homosexuality, and because people's understanding of their sexual orientation can shift over their lives, estimates of the number of lesbian, bisexual, and gay students are quite tentative. However, "most researchers believe that between 5 and 6 percent of youth fit into one of these [lesbian, gay, or bisexual] categories" (Human Rights Watch, 2001, sect. III, p. 1).

The Millennial generation also includes a greater number of transgender students, or at least more students willing to claim this identity. According to Beemyn (2003), "There is no accurate measure of the number of transgender college students. . . . Direct observation and anecdotal evidence suggest that youth who do not fit stereotypical notions of 'female' and 'male' are becoming much more visible on North American campuses and a growing number of students are identifying as gender variant or, as many describe themselves, 'gender queer'" (p. 34).

Little is known about transgender college students, but their needs are gaining greater attention, as more campuses add gender identity and gender expression to their statements of nondiscrimination and still others debate this shift (Transgender Law and Policy Institute, 2003).

Another change evident in this generation is the family structures in which they have been raised. More than any earlier generation, these students come from single-parent families, blended and stepfamilies, and families with same-sex parents. According to Mason and Moulden (1996), "one-fourth of all children born in the U.S. in the early 1980s will live with a step parent before they reach adulthood" (p. 11), and at any given point roughly 25 percent were living with only one parent. Although firm data on the number of children raised by same-sex parents are hard to obtain, several sources indicate that those numbers are significant (between one million and fourteen million, depending on the source consulted) and growing (Cahill, Ellen, and Tobias, 2003). Regardless of the specific numbers, colleges and universities need to reconsider assumptions they make about the family structures of their students, which has implications for financial aid policies, forms, and communication with parents.

Changes in Students' Attitudes Toward Diversity and Social Justice Issues

Millennial students will bring with them not only a different demographic profile from earlier generations but also different views about diversity and social justice issues. Most indicators point toward Millennials having more open attitudes toward issues of diversity and social justice, although there are a number of trends challenging that perspective.

Race and Racism. The Millennial generation has grown up with more mixed messages about race and race relations than perhaps any previous generation. This generation experienced the uprising in South Central Los Angeles in April 1992 following the beating of Rodney King. They witnessed the trial of O. J. Simpson, and how it was perceived by various racial and ethnic groups. Throughout their entire lives, affirmative action has been debated in the media and in the courts. They grew up aware of intense public and governmental attention to illegal immigration, which invariably was cast in racialized terms. As Hu-DeHart (1997) states,

> In short time, illegal aliens ceased to be merely those who enter the country without proper documents. They are the dark-skinned Arab/Muslim religious fundamentalist and terrorist who blows up the World Trade Center in New York City; the black Caribbean sociopath who shoots innocent passengers on the Long Island commuter train; the pregnant Mexican welfare cheat who crosses the border to San Diego to have babies who then become U.S. citizens and in turn enable the mother to claim welfare benefits; the unassimilable Southeast Asian war refugees too eager to take any job at any wage, thus depressing the wage scale and stealing the livelihood of bonafide, longtime Americans [p. 19].

However, this generation, more than any previous, grew up aware of interracial couples, people of color in high-profile governmental positions, and a growing middle class of African Americans, Latinos, and Asian Americans. Overt expressions of racism are increasingly rare on college campuses (Levine and Cureton, 1998), although they certainly still occur.

Indicators of how the Millennial students will view issues of racial and ethnic diversity give a number of messages. Several points, however, are clear. First, though dialogue about race in the United States has historically been primarily a discussion about black and white people, the Millennial generation has a much more expansive understanding of race, one that better reflects the demographics of people of color in the United States. This generation no longer sees race as a black-white issue. It is commonly understood to include Latino and Asian people, and people of all nationalities (Howe and Strauss, 2000).

Less clear is whether the Millennial generation actually has had greater interracial contact than have their predecessors. CIRP data from 2001 indicate that incoming students reported the highest level of cross-race socialization since that question was first asked in 1992 (Sax and others, 2001). However, as discussed earlier, this seems unlikely, given the increasing racial segregation in schools and neighborhoods. This can be explained if demographics are not presumed to be the only reason for contact; perhaps this generation of children is more likely to interact across racial boundaries even if there are fewer other-race children with whom to interact.

Given that conflict around diversity issues is often cited as one of the dominant causes of tension between college students (Levine and Cureton, 1998), these tensions may increase. Additionally, fewer incoming college students see racism as a major problem in America than in the last three years (Sax and others, 2001).

Nevertheless, an increasing number of students are citing more positive attitudes toward race-related issues and support for affirmative action is climbing, although views vary tremendously by race. CIRP data (Sax and others, 2001) indicate that support for the elimination of affirmative action is now at its lowest level (49.0 percent) in the six years the question has been asked. Additionally, also according to 2001 CIRP data, there has been a small rise in interest in working for racial understanding (at 31.5 percent, up from a low of 30.0 percent in 1999, but still far below the high of 46.4 percent in 1992).

Gender and Sexism.   Another area in which Millennial students have different experiences and expectations is that of gender and sexism. This generation holds attitudes about appropriate roles for women that are much more egalitarian than in earlier generations. This is a generation that has seen a rise in women as leaders in peer culture, government (Hillary Clinton, Madeline Albright, and Condoleezza Rice), business, and many other areas. Not surprisingly, "three times more girls than boys now say their top career choice is medicine or law" (Howe and Strauss, 2000, p. 224). As these women enter the university, however, they are likely to notice that women are less evident in the leadership of college campuses; this diversity is not yet reflected in tenure-track faculty and the senior administration of universities (Wenniger and Conroy, 2001).

Millennial students have decreasing expectations that women's place is restricted to the home, with only 21.5 percent of students agreeing that "the activities of women are best restricted to home and family" (Sax and others, 2001, p. 32). At the same time, though, this generation has experienced a much greater level of gender-based segregation in activities, interests, and publications than the one preceding it; men, in particular, are predicted to have trouble redefining their masculinity in socially productive ways (Howe and Strauss, 2000).

Sexual Orientation and Heterosexism.   The Millennial generation has grown up knowing of "out" television and movie stars, politicians, musicians, and possibly peers. They have heard discussions about lesbian, bisexual, and gay people and issues as part of public discourse for their entire lives. Domestic partner benefits, gay marriage, and discussion of gay and lesbian people serving in the military are not new or shocking for many students of the Millennial generation, whether or not they support such policies. Not surprisingly, this generation reflects an increasing level of support for the rights of lesbian and gay people (Sax and others, 2001). This may be a consequence of the increasing number of junior and high school students who are out; the strongest predictor of positive attitudes toward lesbian and gay people is knowingly having had contact with them (Herek, 1997). The Millennial generation shows increasing support for lesbian and gay marriage (57.0 percent of 2001 freshmen believe "same-sex couples should have right to legal marital status," up almost 10 percent from when the question was first asked, in 1997) and decreasing support for criminalization of homosexual relationships, now at a record low level since the question was first asked, in 1976 (Sax and others, 2001).

Reports of harassment and violence at the junior and senior high school levels indicate that these remain exceedingly hostile environments for most lesbian, bisexual, and gay students (Human Rights Watch, 2001), but there also is increasing support for these students and their straight allies. The number of gay-straight alliances in U.S. high schools exceed nine hundred in 2003, spread across forty-six states (Gay, Lesbian, and Straight Education Network, 2003). Students involved in these organizations are likely to bring their growing comfort with lesbian, bisexual, and gay students with them to college.

Political Attitudes. Political views and attitudes about diversity and social justice issues have long been linked, although the relationship has never been exact. Following the Civil War, work to advance social justice issues was more closely linked to liberal political parties than to conservative ones. To some small extent, however, this distinction may be less true of the Millennial generation.

What is clear is that there is an increasing polarization in the political identification of this generation. According to CIRP data, in the entering class of 2001 "those labeling their views as politically 'liberal' or 'far left' [were] at a two decade high" (Sax and others, 2001, p. 2). More students are defining themselves as liberals, but more also are defining themselves as conservatives. In both 2001 and 2002, the percentage of students identifying as conservative rose (Rooney, 2003). According to Colapinto (2003), "The College Republican National Committee, a group that mobilizes students to campaign, has tripled its membership since 1999 to an all-time high of 1,148 chapters" (p. 32). This is challenged somewhat by the findings of the Schneiders/Della Volpe/Schulman group, done in conjunction with Harvard University's Institute of Politics (2003), which asked instead about political party affiliation. They found that although the percentage of students identifying as Democrats has been stable since 2001 (at 29 percent of students in 2001, 2002,and 2003, down from 34 percent in 2000), the fraction of students identifying as Republicans has dropped in the same time frame (from 28 percent in 2000 to 26 percent in both 2002 and 2003). In that same period, however, the percentage of students identifying as independents has grown from 33 percent in 2000 to 41 percent in 2003.

College students' liberalism is evident in a variety of measures, including support for legalization of marijuana along with decreasing support for employer drug-testing of employees or job applicants and for the death penalty. These findings are further supported by the research of the

Schneiders/Della Volpe/Schulman group (2003), which found that regardless of party identification more surveyed college students identified themselves as liberals or moderates (37 percent and 34 percent, respectively) on social issues (including education, health care, and affirmative action) than on general issues (36 percent and 29 percent) or economic issues (25 percent and 42 percent). Nevertheless, according to Colapinto (2003) CIRP data also reflect a conservative shift on a number of other, traditionally liberal issues. Support for the legalization of abortion is down from 66 percent in 1989 to 54 percent in 2002, support for wealthy people paying a larger share of taxes has dropped from 66 percent in 1995 to 50 percent in 2002, and support for gun control laws is at the lowest level ever recorded.

What seems to be occurring is a new definition of liberal and conservative, or at least a distinction between social and economic liberalism and social and economic conservatism. Definitions of what it means to be politically conservative seem to be shifting, particularly around attitudes related to social justice issues; conservative political beliefs no longer can be considered a proxy for racial intolerance. Colapinto (2003) documents leaders of a campus conservative group supporting same-sex unions and saying "People expect us to be like Pat Buchanan, like, 'We're diluting our great Western culture by letting immigrants in.' I don't think any of us buy that" (p. 35). He noted: "Like the rest of their generation, they've been trained, from preschool onward, in the tenets of cooperation, politeness and racial and gender sensitivity. As much as they would hate to admit it—as hard as they try to fight it—these quintessential values have suffused their consciousness and tempered their messages. . . . [The leader of the campus Republican group] has no desire to be mistaken for a bigot" (p. 58).

Social Justice Behaviors. The Millennial generation is likely to engage in behaviors that relate to social justice issues (including voting, community service, protest and demonstrations, and discussion of social and political issues) differently from their predecessors. We can expect them to have a greater focus on social change efforts from within the system, given their tendency to be group-oriented and accepting of authority (Howe and Strauss, 2000). However, this generation seems to be engaging in more visible protest and organizing than recent generations; "participation in organized demonstrations during the past year reached an all-time high 47.5 percent in 2001, compared to 45.4 percent last year and a low of 14.8 percent when this question was first asked in 1966" (Sax and others, 2001, p. 4).

Even though in recent years college students have not been a major force in elections, there is evidence that this is shifting. According to a report by the Schneiders/Della Volpe/Schulman group, 59 percent of college students interviewed stated that they would definitely be voting in the 2004 presidential election, and another 27 percent indicated they probably would vote. Not surprisingly, there has been an increase in entering college students' discussion of politics and belief in maintaining awareness of political affairs (Sax and others, 2001).

This generation has participated in community service and service learning activities at levels unseen in the past; "[the] 2001 [CIRP] survey also marks a record high level of volunteerism, with 82.6 percent of incoming freshmen reporting frequent or occasional volunteer work" (Sax and others, 2001, p. 4). However, recent studies (Jones and Hill, 2003; Marks and Jones, forthcoming) raise the question of whether students will continue their engagement, having absorbed the values that leaders of this movement hope, or whether they will turn away from that which previously has been required of them. The findings of these studies do indicate that those required in high school to serve indeed are less likely to continue their engagement in college than those whose service was voluntary. It is important to remember, also, that not all service activities are closely related to social justice work, although many are.

Implications for Student Affairs Practice

The Millennial generation will ask of and need different things from student affairs practitioners than have previous generations. They will have different demographics, attitudes about diversity issues, and personality characteristics. What follows are some ideas for how we might best prepare for and react to those differences to ensure that all students are welcomed and supported on our campus and that all students learn to work effectively with people unlike themselves.

- *Embrace the reality that our campuses will be different as our students change.* Find ways to incorporate all students, in all aspects of their identities, into the rituals, ceremonies, and cultural aspects of the campus environment. Do not limit their involvement to mere presence; be sure that these aspects of the campus actually incorporate students' cultures, and expect the campus to change along with its students.
- *Be prepared for more sub rosa, less visible conflict around diversity issues.* Conflict is unlikely to manifest in the form of students challenging one another's views, or those of faculty or administrators (Levine and Cureton, 1998). This lack of visible challenge results because this generation is less likely to challenge authority (Howe and Strauss, 2000) and because they have grown up understanding the impact of language, or at least having absorbed the rules about what kinds of issues can and cannot be discussed in formal settings. However, those are exactly the discussions and topics that most need to be explored. Faculty and student affairs staff need to develop settings in which students feel they have license to voice unpopular opinions, be supportively challenged, and articulate the rationale for their positions. Use of technology can facilitate this in some instances, using electronic discussion forums and e-mail lists, although students must assume responsibility for their ideas (that is, posts should not be anonymous). Separate forums can be developed where questions can be

asked anonymously and other students can respond, knowingly participating in settings where they might be offended.

• *Move beyond the "food, festivals, fashion, and fun" approach to diversity.* This generation has grown up with multicultural festivals, international dinners, and "celebrate diversity" messages. We need to help them learn to deal more substantively with issues of power, privilege, and oppression, in both curricular and cocurricular areas. This can be done through formal programming, but also by asking students (and ourselves) questions: "How does your being white affect your work as an RA?" "Do the demographics of your student group represent the campus as a whole? If not, why not? What can you do about it?" "Whom do we picture as our 'normal' student? How do our institutional practices have an impact on students who don't fit that image?"

• *Advocate for curricular diversity requirements that go beyond just learning about international cultures.* Diversity requirements need to deal substantively with how issues of power, privilege, and oppression manifest within the contemporary United States. On many campuses, diversity requirements can be satisfied by courses on non-Western cultures, or on aspects of U.S. history far removed from the present day. These requirements are very important, and students should learn about these cultures and histories. However, it is equally important that they gain a better understanding of how issues of social justice play out in their own country, in the present day.

• *Help students learn to act as allies.* They have learned that difference is good, they know that they should not discriminate, and many are feeling guilty about their privileged social status (Levine and Cureton, 1998). Many students need and want to learn how to work for justice. Develop programming that teaches students to organize groups, to lobby administrators and legislators, and to work with media. Actively recruit students into efforts to create change on issues they care about, be that to participate in rallies, send letters to editors, or question your own administration. Teach them to appropriately challenge their peers' ideas. Role model ally behavior.

• *Identify and address the challenges that students of color face on your campus; assess their needs, challenges, and strengths.* Build on their experience with one another; they will have had far more contact with other students of color than with white students. Be prepared to deal with those who see these efforts as heightening segregation; be able to justify the utility of these programs within the framework of your institution's priorities and mission.

• *Be sure that campus policies and procedures recognize and accommodate the increasing heterogeneity of students.* For example, screen and amend all forms used on campus to be sure they allow all students to accurately reflect their identities, including aspects such as multiple racial identity; nontraditional gender identity; one, two, three, or four parents; parents who are same gender; and so on. Do not presume that all materials sent to parents should be in English. Provide gender-neutral bathrooms and locker room facilities for transgender students. Include gender identity and gender expression in campus nondiscrimination clauses (and sexual orientation, if it does not exist).

• *Be prepared for shifting enrollment patterns in low-income students.* Changes in the need for and availability of financial aid are likely to influence who goes to college; they will shape how and where those students attend. Unless financial aid policies change, or we see a shift in how income is distributed, expect even greater disparity in the enrollment patterns of lower-income students, among whom students of color, immigrants, and first-generation citizens are found in greater numbers. These students will more often attend community colleges, where tuition and fees are lower than at four-year colleges; they will work more hours (up to and beyond forty hours a week) while attending full-time; and fewer students will attend full-time.

The Millennial generation will bring many challenges to student affairs practitioners and faculty, particularly in the area of diversity issues. However, they also are poised to be the generation most able to transform how they, and the larger world, think about and act on these issues. As long as we engage in dialogue with this increasingly diverse generation and make genuine efforts to meet their needs, it should be a productive interaction.

References

Advisory Committee on Student Financial Assistance. "Access Denied: Restoring the Nation's Commitment to Equal Educational Opportunity," 2001. Retrieved Oct. 9, 2003, from http://www.ed.gov/about/bdscomm/list/acsfa/access_denied.pdf.

Battelle Science and Technology International. "Travel Patterns of People of Color. Report Prepared for the Federal Highway Administration," 2000. Retrieved Sept. 20, 2003 from http://www.fhwa.dot.gov/ohim/trvpatns.pdf.

Beemyn, B. "Serving the Needs of Transgender College Students." *Journal of Gay and Lesbian Issues in Education,* 2003, 1(1), 33–50.

Burd, S. "Lack of Need-Based Financial Aid Still Impedes Access to College for Low-Income Students, Report Finds." *Chronicle of Higher Education,* Mar. 2, 2001, p. A26.

Cahill, S., Ellen, M., and Tobias, S. "Family Policy: Issues Affecting Gay, Lesbian, Bisexual and Transgender Families." National Gay and Lesbian Taskforce, 2003. Retrieved Sept. 27, 2003, from http://www.ngltf.org/library/familypolicy.htm.

Camerota, S. "Immigrants in the United States—2002: A Snapshot of America's Foreign-Born Population." Center for Immigration Studies, 2002. Retrieved Oct. 9, 2003 from http://www.cis.org/articles/2002/back1302.pdf.

Carnevale, A. P., and Fry, R. A. *Crossing the Great Divide: Can We Achieve Equity When Generation Y Goes to College?* Washington, D.C.: Educational Testing Service, 2000.

Center on Budget and Policy Priorities. "Two Decades of Extraordinary Gains for Affluent Americans Yield Widest Income Gaps Since 1929, New Data Indicate," 2003. Retrieved Sept. 23, 2003, from http://www.cbpp.org/9–23–03tax-pr.htm.

Colapinto, J. "The Young Hipublicans." *New York Times Magazine,* May 25, 2003, pp. 30–35, 58–59.

Gay, Lesbian, and Straight Education Network. "Issues," 2003. Retrieved Oct. 13, 2003, from http://glsen.org/templates/issues/index.html?subject=3&indepth=1,.

Herek, G. M. "Heterosexuals' Attitudes Toward Lesbians and Gay Men: Does Coming out Make a Difference?" In M. Duberman (ed.), A Queer World: The Center for Lesbian and Gay Studies Reader. New York: New York University, 1997.

Howe, N., and Strauss, W. Millennials Rising: The Next Great Generation. New York: Vintage Books, 2000.

Hu-DeHart, E. "Race, Civil Rights, and the New Immigrants: Nativism and the New World Order." In S. L. Myers, Jr. (ed.), Civil Rights and Race Relations in the Post Reagan-Bush Era. New York: Praeger, 1997.

Human Rights Watch. "Hatred in the Hallways: Violence and Discrimination Against Lesbian, Gay, Bisexual, and Transgender Students in U.S. Schools," 2001. Retrieved Sept. 27, 2003, from http://www.hrw.org/reports/2001/uslbgt/toc.htm.

Jones, S. R., and Hill, K. E. "Understanding Patterns of Commitment: Student Motivation for Community Service Involvement." Journal of Higher Education, 2003, 74, 516–539.

Levine, A., and Cureton, J. "What We Know About Today's College Students." About Campus, 1998, 3(1), 4–9.

Livingston, A., and Wirt, J. The Condition of Education 2003 in Brief. Washington, D.C.: National Center for Education Statistics, 2003. Retrieved Sept. 24, 2003, fromhttp://nces.ed.gov/pubs2003/2003068.pdf.

Logan, J. R. Choosing Segregation: Racial Imbalance in American Public Schools, 1990–2000. Albany: Lewis Mumford Center for Comparative Urban and Regional Research, State University of New York at Albany, 2002. Retrieved Sept. 30, 2003, from http://mumford1.dyndns.org/cen2000/SchoolPop/SPReport/page1.html.

Logan, J. R., and others. Separating the Children. Albany: Lewis Mumford Center for Comparative Urban and Regional Research, State University of New York at Albany, 2001. Retrieved Sept. 30, 2003, from http://mumford1.dyndns.org/cen2000/Under18 Pop/U18Preport/MumfordReport.pdf.

Marks, H. M., and Jones, S. R. "Community Service in the Transition: Shifts and Continuities in Participation from High School to College." Journal of Higher Education, forthcoming.

Mason, M. A., and Moulden, J. "The New Stepfamily Requires New Public Policy." Journal of Social Issues, 1996, 52(3), 11–27.

Pear, R. "Number of People Living in Poverty Increases in U.S." New York Times, Sept. 25, 2002. Retrieved Sept. 25, 2002, from http://www.nytimes.com.

Renn, K. A. Check All That Apply: The Experience of Biracial and Multiracial College Students. Paper presented at the Association for the Study of Higher Education Annual Meeting, Miami, November 1998.

Rooney, M. "Freshmen Showing Rising Political Awareness and Changing Social Views." Chronicle of Higher Education, Jan. 31, 2003, A35–A38.

Rosenblatt, P. "Multiracial Families." In M. E. Lamb (ed.), Parenting and Child Development in "Nontraditional" Families. Hillsdale, N.J.: Erlbaum, 1999.

Sax, L. J., and others. The American Freshman: National Norms for Fall 2001. Los Angeles: Higher Education Research Institute, 2001.

Schneiders/Della Volpe/Schulman. "IOP Spring Survey—Campus Kids: The New Swing Voter." Unpublished report, Schneiders/Della Volpe/Schulman, May 21, 2003.

Transgender Law and Policy Institute. "Schools, Colleges and Universities," 2003. Retrieved from http://transgenderlaw.org/college/#policies.

U.S. Census Bureau. "Census 2000 PHC-T01. Population by Race and Hispanic or Latino Origin, for All Ages and for 18 Years and Over, for the United States: 2000." 2001a. Retrieved Oct. 9, 2003, from http://www.census.gov/population/cen2000/phc-t1/tab01.pdf,.

U.S. Census Bureau. "Profile of the Foreign-Born Population in the United States: 2000. Current Population Reports: Special Studies," 2001b. Retrieved Oct. 9, 2003, from http://www.census.gov/prod/2002pubs/p23–206.pdf.

U.S. Census Bureau. "Census 2000 PHC-T-8: Hispanic or Latino Origin Population; White Alone Not-Hispanic or Latino Origin Population; and Population Other than White Alone Not-Hispanic or Latino Origin, by Age and Sex for the United States: 2000." 2002. Retrieved Oct. 9, 2003, from http://www.census.gov/population/cen2000/phc-t08/tab08.pdf.

Wenniger, M. D., and Conroy, M. H. (eds.). *Gender Equity or Bust!: On the Road to Campus Leadership with Women in Higher Education.* San Francisco: Jossey-Bass, 2001.

ELLEN M. BROIDO is assistant professor of higher education and student affairs at Bowling Green State University in Ohio.

This chapter examines the Millennial generation's implications for the design and delivery of student affairs programs and services. The unique characteristics of the Millennial students offer insights into the programs and services that this generation of college students will want and need.

Student Affairs for a New Generation

John Wesley Lowery

As noted in the previous chapters of this sourcebook, the Millennial generation represents a significant departure from the immediately preceding Thirteenth generation, or Generation X, and is a correction for the excesses of the Boomer generation. Howe and Strauss (2000) identify seven key characteristics of the Millennial generation: special, sheltered, confident, team-oriented, conventional, pressured, and achieving. These characteristics have significant implications for the design and delivery of student affairs programs and services. They also suggest new patterns and levels of student involvement in campus life that have not been seen at colleges and universities for a number of years. This and future generations will also require a reexamination of how programs and services are organized and delivered. This chapter addresses those issues and concludes by offering insights into establishing a model for the division of student affairs that is flexible enough to be responsive to new generations of students.

Millennials and Student Affairs

Newton (2000) describes the Millennial students coming to college as "a new *breed* of students on campus" (p. 9). These Millennial students are facing the same developmental issues and challenges as previous generations, but they have grown up in a world fundamentally different from that of their predecessors (Howe and Strauss, 1993, 2000, 2003; Newton, 2000; Strauss and Howe, 1991). The unique characteristics of the Millennial generation offer insights into the programs and services that these students will need as well as the design and delivery of student affairs programs and services.

Special. Throughout their lives, the Millennial generation has served as a central focus of society's positive attention (Howe and Strauss, 2000). One of the personal manifestations of this specialness is the relationship that many Millennial students enjoy with their parents. Many Millennials consider their parents to be one of their role models whose involvement in their lives they embrace (O'Briant, 2003). This involvement is so extensive that the college application process is understood by both parents and students as a "co-purchasing" (Howe and Strauss, 2003, p. 69) decision. An entire industry has emerged to assist parents and students to manage the admissions process, and to help ensure that students are able to attend the right college (Schneider and Stevenson, 1999). Another segment of this new industry claims to help parents identify the financial resources needed to pay tuition once their children are admitted (Hoover, 2003). Strauss observes:

> The number one thing to realize with the Millennials is that as a whole they reflect much more parental perfectionism than any generation in living memory. Colleges and universities should know that they are not just getting a kid but they are also getting a parent. The college decision is a co-purchase decision more than ever before. More than Gen Xers at that age, today's teens get along with their parents, they rely on their parents, they share their parents' attitudes and values although they may consider themselves as a more pure embodiment of those values than the parents, because they're prepared to actually live by the values whereas Boomers are not perceived as being particularly good at that [in Lowery, 2001, p. 8].

Many student affairs administrators have reported a significant increase in recent years in the amount of parent-initiated contact with colleges and universities (Forbes, 2001). Parental involvement begins with the recruitment and admissions process, but it certainly does not end there. As Strauss warns, "From the admissions process all the way through the college experience expect there to be more parental involvement and support—and more parental intrusion and annoyance. Colleges will find ways to marshal the parents to do things that are helpful. Parents will be sending e-mails to professors and presidents and what not, who may want to construct walls with 'Keep Away' signs for parents" (in Lowery, 2001, p. 8).

It is incumbent on student affairs professionals to create opportunities for parents to be involved in their students' education without removing the role of college as a place where students develop the ability to live independently from their parents. Howe and Strauss (2003) note "this means that colleges and universities must negotiate carefully with parents, manage their expectations, and understand that many of them may be experiencing their own rite of passage" (p. 70). One means of creating these opportunities is to partner with parents to address difficult issues on campus proactively. Forbes (2001) describes efforts at Lafayette College to involve parents in the institution's alcohol and drug abuse prevention efforts. Institutions can also respond effectively to parental involvement by developing resources about institutional policies specifically for parents and by carefully explaining to parents the institution's limitations in sharing information with parents about their students.

Sheltered. Society has demonstrated its concern for the Millennials with efforts to protect them from every conceivable harm. Howe and Strauss (2000) describe the Millennials as "the focus of the most sweeping youth safety movement in American history" (p. 43). On campus we have seen a marked increase in concern over campus crime and demands that institutions respond swiftly and decisively to student misconduct. These calls for campus safety only increased in the wake of the terrorist attacks of September 11 and the subsequent war on Iraq.

One of the ironies of this new parental involvement is that Millennials' parents, many of whom are boomers, are members of the generation that helped usher in the end of *in loco parentis* on campus (Shapiro, 2002). Graham Spanier, president of Pennsylvania State University, observes, "They [parents] want in loco parentis" (Bronner, 1999, p. 1). The rules for Millennials have always been clearly articulated, with minimal opportunity for interpretation or debate about their meaning or scope. However, unlike their Generation X forebears, Millennial students have not rebelled against these heightened expectations for their behavior. Howe and Strauss (2000) observe, "Here, too, as with much else, this rising generation is growing up accustomed to the task of meeting and beating standards older people couldn't—and often still can't—handle themselves" (p. 212). One of the most striking examples has proven to be their unquestioning acceptance of parental notification policies for alcohol and drug violations. Many college administrators scratch their heads in surprise that there has not been more outrage and protest from undergraduates. However, this seems less surprising in light of the results of the Uhlich National Teen Report Card on Adults (Uhlich Children's Advantage Network, 2003), in which teens gave adults failing grades for their ability to stop teen drinking and drug abuse.

Although the Millennial generation is arguably the healthiest youth generation in recent memory, society and the media seem unaware of this positive outcome. In many areas (for example, drunk driving, teenage pregnancy, violence in schools, and suicide), Millennials seem to be headed in a positive direction. It should be noted that some significant health issues have increased in recent years, including ADHD, sports-related injuries, and obesity. This is coupled with a Millennial generation that has been conditioned to seek the help of adults in dealing with its problems, large and small. Counseling center directors are reporting a significant increase in the number of students taking psychiatric medications as well as the number of students with severe psychiatric problems (Benton and others, 2003; Young, 2003a). These students may place even greater demands on counseling centers, student health centers, and student affairs staff in general (Howe and Strauss, 2003; Sax, 2003; Schneider and Stevenson, 1999).

The combination of these first two characteristics, special and sheltered, may help explain a general concern shared by many student affairs professionals. Repeatedly, student affairs professionals complain about Millennial students and their parents who immediately call the vice president's office or the president's office to seek resolution of the smallest complaints—often without ever attempting to resolve the issue through appropriate institutional structures. For example, a mother calls the president's office to express concern about her son's conflict with his roommate as her first step to resolve the conflict. Institutions first need to educate students and parents about the appropriate avenues for resolving issues that commonly occur. Perhaps even more important, institutions should create systems so that upper-level administrators can quickly reroute these issues to the appropriate office on campus and encourage those administrators to reinforce the importance of attempting to resolve the issue through the normal process.

Confident. Unlike the bleak future foreseen by the members of Generation X (Copeland, 1991; Holtz, 1995; Howe and Strauss, 1993), the Millennials look toward the future longingly, confident in the knowledge that they have the capacity to be the next greatest generation (Howe and Strauss, 2000, 2003). Sax (2003) observes that these Millennial students have "grown increasingly optimistic about their chances for success in college" (p. 17). For example, the percentage of students predicting they will graduate with honors has increased fivefold over the past thirty years. However, Schneider and Stevenson (1999) observe that these ambitious students do not have a clear plan for how to achieve these goals. Although Millennials report stronger academic performance, these students are not as committed to studying and homework (Sax, 2003). Sax warns that their unrealistic academic expectations may lead students to "become demoralized when they earn their first B or C grade" (p. 19). These students will need support from student affairs professionals to develop meaningful and realistic plans to achieve their ambitious goals, and they will require support when their performance does not meet their own expectations.

Another source of confidence for Millennials is their technological expertise. Newton (2000) observes, "Students today are on the cutting edge of technological proficiency, and in most cases they are beyond their parents, teachers, and potential bosses" (p. 11). This technological proficiency, fostered by the computers in their bedrooms and cell phones in their pockets, has developed in this generation the marked ability to multitask (Lancaster and Stillman, 2002; Zemke, Raines, and Filipczak, 2000).

However, their comfort with and constant use of technology is not without its dark side. Barnard (2003) is concerned that steady use of cell phones makes the task of building community on campus more difficult as face-to-face discussions have been replaced with chatting on the phone. The combination of cell phones and ubiquitous instant messaging (IM) programs allows students to remain in much more direct contact with parents as well as friends from high school who are still at home or are attending other colleges. This may prove to be an obstacle to students developing friendships and community at college. Furthermore, students often use these technologies to communicate with other students, preferring to e-mail the student down the hall rather than walking to his or her room to talk (Blimling, 2000). There is a value in this type of communication, though. Putnam, Feldstein, and Cohen (2003) observe, "E-ties to people who you also know offline constitute a kind of alloy that combines the advantages of both computer-based and face-to-face connections" (p. 226). However, this is only true if e-ties supplement, not supplant, face-to-face connections.

Part of the ritual of going to college in the past was a separation from former relationships, including friends and parents. However, new technology "is making it harder for Millennials to 'let go' of their old high school worlds, to replace old friends with new ones" (Howe and Strauss, 2003, p. 93). One institution went so far as to ban cell phone use during a portion of the orientation program to encourage students to make connections on campus (Barnard, 2003). Institutions can also take advantage of students' comfort with this type of technology to help make connections on campus. For example, the University of South Carolina uses its Blackboard course management system to create virtual communities alongside the institution's physical residence hall communities. These virtual communities can "strengthen, broaden, and deepen existing personal ties" (Putnam, Feldstein, and Cohen, 2003, p. 226).

Team-Oriented. Unlike the individualistic orientation of generation X, the Millennials evidence a strong team orientation, which has been reinforced by parents and in schools throughout their lives (Howe and Strauss, 2000, 2003). Millennials seem most comfortable in group activities and in group settings. The attraction of group work includes the opportunity not only to demonstrate their cooperativeness but also to reduce the risk of individual failure (Howe and Strauss, 2000; Lancaster and Stillman, 2002).

A consequence of these experiences is a strong preference by Millennials for structured rather than unstructured activities. Millennials often seem to lack the tolerance for ambiguity that older generations regarded as an important strength (Howe and Strauss, 2003). The two student affairs areas affected by this need for structure are orientation and leadership development programs. Millennials place significant importance upon a structured training that focuses on what to do as well as an explanation of the reasoning behind it (Lancaster and Stillman, 2002).

This team orientation may also serve as a partial explanation of the Millennials' extensive involvement in community service. Admittedly, part of the explanation rests in service requirements at the high school level. However, many of these students participated in high school service without any requirement (Howe and Strauss, 2000; Sax, 2003). Sax notes that this involvement in service did not take place in the context of political or social activism; rather, it was rooted in a desire and belief in their ability to improve their own communities—not to change the country, or the world. Some commentators have described their participation in service as grounded in a desire to improve their resumes, rather than their communities (Newton, 2000). However, at least some concern about developing a strong portfolio of experience to help students move successfully into the next phase of their lives should not be surprising, given their parents' emphasis on building "extensive portfolios for college admission" (Lancaster and Stillman, 2002, p. 65). Student affairs professionals may be able to harness the Millennials' portfolio mentality to reinvigorate the cocurricular or student development transcript model that enjoyed some modest popularity in the late 1970s and early 1980s (Brown and Citrin, 1977, Bryan, Mann, Nelson, and North, 1981).

The strong team orientation of Millennials presents several challenges to student affairs professionals. Their team orientation can give way to groupthink, which suppresses individuality (Howe and Strauss, 2000). Their desire to work in a cooperative environment can lead these students to avoid confrontation situations and difficult students. These Millennials need help to develop the skills necessary to effectively respond to conflict in personal and organizational settings (Lancaster and Stillman, 2002). For example, residence life staff need to devote considerable energy to help students effectively manage roommate conflicts and challenge students to work to resolve these conflicts rather than simply seeking to have a third party resolve it for them. Finally, student affairs professionals must continue to be on the lookout for students who have not been able to find their niche or community on campus. This has always been a focus for student affairs, but the Millennials' team and community focus makes this challenge even more important. Howe and Strauss (2003) warn that the issue may be particularly important in the case of male students, who seem more likely to face this particular challenge. Chickering and Reisser (1993) warn that "male students may have more difficulty forming friendships, especially with other men" (p. 170).

Conventional. In many ways, the Millennials are accurately described as neotraditionalists who represent the most conservative youth culture in recent memory (Howe and Strauss, 2000). Howe and Strauss (2003) suggest that the traditionalism of this generation may see a return of campus spirit last seen just before the emergence of the student protest movement in the 1960s. As Howe and Strauss (2003) suggest, "Many Millennials will reveal what their edgier elders might demean as 'corny-cultural' values, a modernized rebirth of pep rallies, awards ceremonies, school songs, proms, and the like" (p. 88). Strauss is encouraged by this traditionalism: "You will see on campus a push toward a new traditionalism where students want to have a college experience in the classic sense. I think that college administrators will enjoy wrapping this around them" (in Lowery, 2001, p. 9).

A number of commentators (see, for instance, Howe and Strauss, 2000; Lancaster and Stillman, 2002) have also commented on a return to manners by the Millennials as further evidence of their conventional nature. Adults may be surprised by this assertion, given the portrayal of Millennials in the media and the behavior and dress of some of their icons such as Britney Spears and Christina Aguilera. However, these students are often more modest about their own bodies than images in the popular culture would suggest. Zemke, Raines, and Filipczak (2000) point out that their manners are just one of many points of comparison between the Millennial generation and GI or veteran generation.

As a result of the Millennial generation's team orientation and willingness to embrace conventional values, student affairs professionals will likely see a renewed interest in large, campuswide programs, which fell out of favor in recent decades. Strauss sees great potential in these students to reshape campus life. As he urges, "Let collegians do creative things, and help them generate audiences and collaborators. If you succeed at this, you could have all kinds of exciting things happening on campus, where collegians are busy producing things that contribute to everyone's college experience" (in Lowery, 2001, p. 11).

Institutions should also take this into consideration when designing campus facilities, to provide multiuse spaces that allow small and large group events (Moneta, 2003).

Pressured. The societal messages about the special nature of the Millennials and their role as the next great generation place much pressure on them to shape our society in the years to come. However, their experiences in high school have exposed them to a previously unseen level of pressure. These students have experienced highly scheduled lives for years and considerable pressure to get into the right college. Newton (2000) notes that "emotionally, students are experiencing increasingly high levels of stress and anxiety" (p. 10). In an article titled "The Organization Kid," Brooks (2001) describes how involved these new students are in campus life: "I asked several students to describe their daily schedules, and their replies sounded like a session of Future Workaholics of America: crew practice at dawn, classes in the morning, resident-adviser duty, lunch, study groups, classes in the afternoon, tutoring disadvantaged kids in Trenton, a cappella practice, dinner, science lab, prayer session, hit the StairMaster, study a few hours more" (p. 40).

However, he also concludes that the involvement of these new students is goal-oriented rather than focused on financial success, as was the case with previous generations of students. Another source of pressure for these students is concern about paying for college. Sax (2003) notes that about two-thirds of these students are worried about paying for college, and almost half expect to work during college to help pay those costs.

There are several ways in which student affairs administrators can assist Millennial students in this regard. First, workshops and training should be offered to help these students effectively manage this pressure, and opportunities should be created to relieve it. Students also need help developing realistic expectations about their own capacity for work. Although Millennial students speak often about a desire for balance on campus and in the workplace, they are seldom successful in achieving it (Howe and Strauss, 2003; Lancaster and Stillman, 2002). Within this pressured environment, students may experience "occasional periods of 'burnout'" (Howe and Strauss, 2003, p. 117) during which they effectively shut down. As Lancaster and Stillman note, if you forget to turn the heat down on the pressure cooker, it is going to explode. Newton (2000) advises that "students need to have skills to manage their daily lives" (p. 14) and recommends that institutions seek to develop and market programs to help students develop self-management skills in such areas as time management, financial issues, relationships, and dealing with stress.

Another concern born of the pressure placed upon the Millennial student is the issue of academic dishonesty. The enhanced pressured to succeed and the impact on self-esteem of academic performance that does not meet expectations is one explanation of why college students cheat (Kibler and Kibler, 1993). One area in which institutions must make considerable effort is plagiarism. The same technology that these students have mastered so fully has also proven a powerful tool for plagiarism. Howe and Strauss (2003) point out that many of these students received significant help from their parents in writing their college admissions essays, and in some cases even papers assigned in college. As a generation, Millennials have also grown up in a culture where a clear sense of who created intellectual products is not valued or understood. Results of the 2003 National Survey of Student Engagement (NSSE) found that 87 percent of students surveyed said they were aware of fellow students who had copied information from the Internet and included it in their papers without proper attribution (Young, 2003b). One method for addressing this concern is to take active steps to ensure that all students clearly understand what is acceptable and what is not to avoid problems with plagiarism (Howe and Strauss, 2003). Institutions would be well advised to seek out multiple avenues for communicating this important message, including orientation programs, first-year seminar courses, and courses by instructors across the curriculum. Institutions may also be able to successfully tap into these students' willingness to embrace tradition and desire for community to address this growing problem. Successes enjoyed through the use of social norms marketing to address alcohol and drug abuse may hold promise in other areas of concern for just this reason (Newton, 2000).

Achieving. The Millennials have consistently received messages about their academic achievements. Howe and Strauss (2003) are particularly positive about this generation, proclaiming that "Millennials are smart—and getting smarter by the year. They are probably the most all-around capable teenage generation this nation, and perhaps the world, has ever seen" (p. 123).

This last Millennial characteristic is best understood in light of the first characteristic discussed in this chapter. Millennials have repeatedly been told that they are special and that great things are expected of their generation. Sax (2003) cautions, however, against overemphasizing this trend because of concerns over grade inflation in high school for more than three decades. Both inside and outside of the classroom, Millennials will question and reject subjective methods of evaluation, seeking instead more objective systems of grading that leave no room for doubt about the appropriateness of their final grade. In receiving grades or decisions considered unacceptable, Millennials and their parents are more willing than previous generations to vocally challenge the system—even if it means going to court to resolve the issues (Howe and Strauss, 2003). A wise first step in addressing this concern is to develop well-written and clearly communicated internal policies for grade appeals.

Delivery of Services

The demands that the Millennial generation will place upon higher education require reconsideration not only of the services they are provided but also of the means by which these services are delivered. These students have grown up in a world of instant gratification. The infusion of technology into their lives has reduced the time required to complete seemingly any task. Delays in response longer than the Millennials consider appropriate, however unrealistic, result in the perception that their issues or needs are not valued. Recognizing students' expectation for rapid replies, the Stevens Institute of Technology requires faculty to reply to all student e-mails within forty-eight hours (Young, 2002). The business sector has recognized the impact of this generation's expectation for rapid replies as well; Lancaster and Stillman (2002) report the efforts of some companies to significantly reduce the time required to make a decision in a job search.

The use of technology, which is second nature to Millennials, holds the greatest promise for responding to their preference for efficient services. In fact, Millennial students will demand it. Blimling (2000) observes that "students come to college expecting technological sophistication" (p. 4). One of the benefits of using technology to deliver services is the potential of twenty-four-hour access to services. Levine and Cureton (1998) suggest that students will expect and demand this type of relationship with their institution—whether a bank or a university. The use of technology can also contribute to the student's experience; the results of the 2003 NSSE suggest that effective use of technology can improve student engagement (Young, 2003b).

Even though most institutions have developed basic services on the Internet, there are still significant opportunities for developing advanced, interactive Web-based technologies. Cawthon, Havice, and Havice (2003) describe how Clemson University developed an online system for providing academic advising using webcams, a technology that may be new to faculty members and administrators but is well within the Millennials' comfort zone. Other examples include development of expanded career center services for 24/7 student access (Dodson and Dean, 2003) and online student activities programming (Conway and Hubbard, 2003).

There is a tendency to associate online student services with those students participating in distance learning opportunities. However, these services will also be appealing to and used by on-campus students (Krauth and Carbajal, 2002). Kendall, Smith, Moore, and Oaks (2001) suggest these components of online student services are critical:

- A convenient, any-time/any-place delivery modality, which implies an asynchronous system, part of which should be a self-service model
- One-stop shopping, which means student service staffs must be trained across functions and able to address at least the first five or eight questions about every element of a program
- Services equal in quality and diversity to those provided on campus
- Services based on identified needs of distance learners, which means that we need ongoing feedback loops and that we need to be willing to adjust our services when needs change
- Ways to ensure that distance students feel connected to their institution

Howe and Strauss (2003) also urged student affairs professionals to tap into the potential of the Millennial students themselves to reshape the college campus. The authors suggest that "student governments (and judiciaries) will assume new importance, especially if college administrators expand their authority over student rules, discipline, campus activities, and community service" (p. 100). For example, one new approach to disciplinary problems on campus that Millennial students may embrace is restorative justice, which seeks to repair harm to the community resulting from students' actions (Lowery and Dannells, forthcoming).

Organizing Student Affairs Work

Unfortunately, there is not a single organizational structure that is guaranteed to meet the needs of the Millennial generation and work for all institutions. Woodward, Love, and Komives note a dominant myth of student affairs, that "there is one correct organizational model for student affairs" (2000, p. 62). Furthermore, the authors argue that many "student affairs practitioners believe that rethinking or restructuring an organization, division, or department is not productive and is a waste of time" (p. 62). Though not offering a single organizational model for student affairs, Woodward, Love, and Komives present this advice for practitioners as they work to establish an organizational structure:

- Assess the environment
- Seek advice and alliances
- Watch out for danger signs
- Pay attention to the analysis
- Watch out for a not-in-my-backyard attitude
- Take care of business (2000, pp. 67–69)

One thing that should be carefully considered in the process of determining the most effective organization model for any institution of higher education is the student body's characteristics. Sandeen (2001) predicts that "the best student affairs organizations will reflect these special populations and engage in regular assessment so that they can understand and adapt to the inevitable changes that occur" (p. 190).

In the coming years, new organizational models must be developed to incorporate the work styles of Millennial employees and to address the needs of the Millennial students they serve. Zemke, Raines, and Filipczak (2000) suggest that organizations will have to spend considerably more time orienting Millennial employees and need to be certain to provide for ongoing training and development programs. Zemke, Raines, and Filipczak (2000) also advocate that when creating work teams consisting of Millennials careful consideration be given to appointing a strong team leader or unit head. Millennials will want more supervision and structure than their Generation X predecessors. There have been significant complaints from Boomers in recent years about the lack of a meaningful work ethic on the part of Generation X employees. Millennials may find this criticism leveled at them, although they are more likely to express the problem as one of finding balance in their lives. Lancaster and Stillman (2002) urge businesses to develop and expand flexible scheduling or comp time programs, which allow employees to find some measure of the balance they seek.

Conclusion

Strauss predicts that, "done right, we could see a new golden age of campuses. By the end of this decade, Millennials may well transform the American campus as much as Boomers did in the sixties, but they will transform it in the opposite direction" (in Lowery, 2001, p. 11). However, commentators such as Sax (2003) and Newton (2000) identify issues with this new generation that are bound to be troubling to student affairs professionals and demand careful attention.

Armed with a greater understanding of and appreciation for the unique characteristics of the Millennial generation and the services they will demand as a result, student affairs professionals are better prepared to help this new generation reach their potential. In the years to come, student affairs must also redesign the workplace as the Millennial generation comes to dominate the campus both as students and as student affairs professionals. Student affairs professionals can also aid campuses by helping the broader campus community better understand these new students.

References

Barnard, C. A. "The Impact of Cell Phone Use on Building Community." *Student Affairs Online,* 2003, *4*(4). Retrieved Nov. 4, 2003, from http://studentaffairs.com/ejournal/Fall_2003/CellPhones.html.

Benton, S. A., Robertson, J. M., Tseng, W., Newton, F. B., and Benton, S. L. "Changes in Counseling Center Client Problems Across 13 Years." *Professional Psychology: Research and Practice,* 2003, *34,* 66–72.

Blimling, G. S. "New Technologies: Changing How We Work with Students." *About Campus,* 2000, *5*(4), 3–7.

Bronner, E. "In a Revolution on Campus Rules, Campuses Go Full Circle." *New York Times,* Mar. 3, 1999, pp. 1, 15.

Brooks, D. "The Organization Kid." *Atlantic Monthly.* Apr. 2001, pp. 40–54.

Brown, R. D., and Citrin, R. S. "A Student Development Transcript: Assumptions, Uses, and Formats." *Journal of College Student Development,* 1977, *40,* 504–509.

Bryan, W. A., Mann, G. T., Nelson, R. B., and North, R. A. "The Co-Curricular Transcript: What Do Employers Think? A National Survey." *NASPA Journal,* 1981, *19*(1), 29–36.

Cawthon, T. W., Havice, P. A., and Havice, W. L. "Enhancing Collaboration in Student Affairs: Virtual Advising." *Student Affairs Online,* 2003, *4*(4). Retrieved Nov. 4, 2003, from http://studentaffairs.com/ejournal/Fall_2003/VirtualAdvising.html.

Chickering, A. W., and Reisser, L. *Education and Identity* (2nd ed.). San Francisco: Jossey-Bass, 1993.

Conway, J., and Hubbard, B. "From Bricks to Bytes: Building an Online Activities Environment." *Student Affairs Online,* 2003, *4*(3). Retrieved from Nov. 4, 2003, http://studentaffairs.com/ejournal/Summer_2003/Bricks-to-Bytes.html.

Copeland, D. *Generation X.* New York: St. Martin's Press, 1991.

Dodson, L. F., and Dean, M. "Career Services 24/7: The Online Career Center." *Student Affairs Online,* 2003, *4*(3). Retrieved Nov. 4, 2003, from http://studentaffairs.com/ejournal/Summer_2003/CareerServices24–7.html.

Forbes, K. J. "Students and Their Parents: Where Do Campuses Fit in?" *About Campus,* Sept./Oct. 2001, pp. 11–17.

Holtz, G. T. *Welcome to the Jungle: The Why Behind "Generation X."* New York: St. Martin's Press, 1995.

Hoover, E. "Pushing the Envelope." *Chronicle of Higher Education,* Oct. 17, 2003, pp. A39-A42.

Howe, N., and Strauss, W. *13th Gen: Abort, Retry, Ignore, Fail?* New York: Vintage Books, 1993.

Howe, N., and Strauss, W. *Millennials Rising: The Next Great Generation.* New York: Vintage Books, 2000.

Howe, N., and Strauss, W. *Millennials Go to College.* Great Falls, Va.: American Association of Collegiate Registrars and LifeCourse Associates, 2003.

Kendall, J. R., Smith, C., Moore, R., and Oaks, M. "Student Services for Distance Learners: A Critical Component." *Netresults: NASPA's E-zine for Student Affairs Professionals,* Apr. 9, 2001. Retrieved from Nov. 4, 2003, http://www.naspa.org/membership/mem/nr/article.cfm?id=229.

Kibler, W. L., and Kibler, P. V. "When Students Resort to Cheating: Colleges Need a Comprehensive Approach to Academic Dishonesty." *Chronicle of Higher Education,* July 14, 1993, pp. B1-B2.

Krauth, B., and Carbajal, J. "Guide to Developing Online Student Services." *Netresults: NASPA's E-zine for Student Affairs Professionals,* Feb. 6, 2002. Retrieved Nov. 4, 2003, from http://www.naspa.org/membership/mem/nr/article.cfm?id=587.

Lancaster, L. C., and Stillman, D. *When Generations Collide.* New York: HarperBusiness, 2002.

Levine, A., and Cureton, J. S. *When Hope and Fear Collide: A Portrait of Today's College Student.* San Francisco: Jossey-Bass, 1998.

Lowery, J. W. "The Millennials Come to College: John Wesley Lowery Talks with William Strauss." *About Campus,* 2001, *6*(3), 6–12.

Lowery, J. W., and Dannells, M. "Contemporary Practice in Student Judicial Affairs: Strengths and Weaknesses." In D. A. Karp and T. Allena (eds.), *Restorative Community Justice on the College Campus.* Springfield, Ill.: Charles C. Thomas, forthcoming.

Moneta, L. "Future Trends and Challenges for Student Affairs: A Senior Student Affairs Officer's Perspective. *Leadership Exchange,* Spring 2003, pp. 6–9.

Newton, F. B. "The New Student." *About Campus,* 2000, *5*(5), 8–15.

O'Briant, D. "Millennials: The Next Generation." *Atlanta Journal Constitution,* Aug. 11, 2003. Retrieved Oct. 20, 2003, from http://www.ajc.com.

Putnam, R. D., Feldstein, L. M., and Cohen, D. *Better Together: Restoring the American Community.* New York: Simon and Schuster, 2003.

Sandeen, A. "Organizing Student Affairs Divisions." In R. B. Winston Jr., D. G. Creamer, and T. K. Miller (eds.), *The Professional Student Affairs Administrator.* New York: Brunner-Routledge, 2001.

Sax, L. J. "Our Incoming Students: What Are They Like?" *About Campus,* 2003, *8*(3), 15–20.

Schneider, B., and Stevenson, D. *The Ambitious Generation: America's Teenagers, Motivated But Directionless.* New Haven, Conn.: Yale University Press, 1999.

Shapiro, J. R. "Keeping Parents off Campus." *New York Times,* Aug. 22, 2002, p. 23.

Strauss, W., and Howe, N. *Generations: The History of America's Future, 1584 to 2069.* New York: Morrow, 1991.

Uhlich Children's Advantage Network. "Uhlich National Teen Report Card on Adults," 2003. Retrieved from Oct. 20, 2003, http://www.ucanchicago.org/reportcard.

Woodward, D. B., Love, P., and Komives, S. R. *Leadership and Management Issues for a New Century.* San Francisco: Jossey-Bass, 2000.

Young, J. R. "The 24-Hour Professor: Online Teaching Redefines Faculty Members' Schedules, Duties, and Relationships with Students." *Chronicle of Higher Education,* May 31, 2002, pp. A31-A33.

Young, J. R. "Prozac Campus: More Students Seek Counseling and Take Psychiatric Medication." *Chronicle of Higher Education,* Feb. 14, 2003a, p. A37.

Young, J. R. "Student 'Engagement' in Learning Varies Significantly by Major, Survey Finds." *Chronicle of Higher Education,* Nov. 14, 2003b, p. A37.

Zemke, R., Raines, C., and Filipczak, R. *Generations at Work: Managing the Clash of Veterans, Boomers, Xers, and Nexters in Your Workplace.* New York: AMACOM, 2000.

JOHN WESLEY LOWERY is assistant professor of higher education and student affairs in the Department of Educational Leadership and Policies at the University of South Carolina. He previously held administrative positions at Adrian College and Washington University.

Index

Back Issue/Subscription Order Form

Copy or detach and send to:
Jossey-Bass, A Wiley Imprint, 989 Market Street, San Francisco CA 94103-1741

Call or fax toll-free: Phone 888-378-2537 6:30AM – 3PM PST; Fax 888-481-2665

Back Issues: Please send me the following issues at $27 each
(Important: please include ISBN number with your order.)

_____

_____

_____

$ _____   Total for single issues

$ _____   SHIPPING CHARGES: SURFACE   Domestic Canadian
                                    First Item $5.00 $6.00
                                    Each Add'l Item $3.00 $1.50
                 For next-day and second-day delivery rates, call the number listed above.

Subscriptions   Please __ start __ renew my subscription to *New Directions for Student Services* for the year 2_____at the following rate:

U.S.	__ Individual $75	__ Institutional $160
Canada	__ Individual $75	__ Institutional $200
All Others	__ Individual $99	__ Institutional $234
Online Subscription		__ Institutional $160

**For more information about online subscriptions visit
www.interscience.wiley.com**

$ _____   Total single issues and subscriptions (Add appropriate sales tax for your state for single issue orders. No sales tax for U.S. subscriptions. Canadian residents, add GST for subscriptions and single issues.)

__Payment enclosed (U.S. check or money order only)
__VISA __ MC __ AmEx __ Card #_____Exp.Date_____

Signature _____ Day Phone _____
__Bill Me (U.S. institutional orders only. Purchase order required.)

Purchase order # _____
                 Federal Tax ID13559302   **GST 89102 8052**

Name _____

Address _____

_____

Phone _____ E-mail _____

For more information about Jossey-Bass, visit our Web site at www.josseybass.com

grounds, and that student affairs professionals make valuable contributions to the success of campus facility projects. Covers planning, budgeting, collaboration, and communication through case studies and lessons learned. ISBN: 0-7879-6847-1

SS100   **Student Affairs and External Relations**
Mary Beth Snyder
Building positive relations with external constituents is as important in student affairs work as it is in any other university or college division. This issue is a long-overdue resource of ideas, strategies, and information aimed at making student affairs leaders more effective in their interactions with important off-campus partners, supporters, and agencies. Chapter authors explore the current challenges facing the student services profession as well as the emerging opportunities worthy of student affairs interest.
ISBN: 0-7879-6342-9

SS99   **Addressing Contemporary Campus Safety Issues**
Christine K. Wilkinson, James A. Rund
Provided for practitioners as a resource book for both historical and evolving issues, this guide covers hazing, parental partnerships, and collaborative relationships between universities and the neighboring community. Addressing a new definition of a safe campus environment, the editors have identified topics such as the growth in study abroad, the implications of increased usage of technology on campus, and campus response to September 11. In addition, large-scale crisis responses to student riots and multiple campus tragedies have been described in case studies. The issue speaks to a more contemporary definition of a safe campus environment that addresses not only physical safety issues but also those of a psychological nature, a more diverse student body, and quality of life.
ISBN: 0-7879-6341-0

SS98   **The Art and Practical Wisdom of Student Affairs Leadership**
Jon Dalton, Marguerite McClinton
This issue collects reflections, stories, and advice about the art and practice of student affairs leadership. Ten senior student affairs leaders were asked to maintain a journal and record their personal reflections on practical wisdom they have gained in the profession. The authors looked inside themselves to provide personal and candid insight into the convictions and values that have guided them in their work and lives.
ISBN: 0-7879-6340-2

SS97   **Working with Asian American College Students**
*Marylu K. McEwen, Corinne Maekawa Kodama, Alvin N. Alvarez, Sunny Lee,
Christopher T. H. Liang*
Highlights the diversity of Asian American college students, analyzes the "model minority" myth and the stereotype of the "perfidious foreigner," and points out the need to consider the racial identity and racial consciousness of Asian American students. Various authors propose a model of Asian American student development, address issues of Asian Americans who are at educational risk, discuss the importance of integration and collaboration between student affairs and Asian American studies programs, and offer strategies for developing socially conscious Asian American student leaders.
ISBN: 0-7879-6292-9S

NEW DIRECTIONS FOR STUDENT SERVICES IS NOW AVAILABLE ONLINE AT WILEY INTERSCIENCE

What is Wiley InterScience?

Wiley InterScience is the dynamic online content service from John Wiley & Sons delivering the full text of over 300 leading scientific, technical, medical, and professional journals, plus major reference works, the acclaimed *Current Protocols* laboratory manuals, and even the full text of select Wiley print books online.

What are some special features of Wiley InterScience?

Wiley InterScience Alerts is a service that delivers table of contents via e-mail for any journal available on Wiley InterScience as soon as a new issue is published online.
Early View is Wiley's exclusive service presenting individual articles online as soon as they are ready, even before the release of the compiled print issue. These articles are complete, peer-reviewed, and citable.
CrossRef is the innovative multi-publisher reference linking system enabling readers to move seamlessly from a reference in a journal article to the cited publication, typically located on a different server and published by a different publisher.

How can I access Wiley InterScience?

Visit http://www.interscience.wiley.com

Guest Users can browse Wiley InterScience for unrestricted access to journal Tables of Contents and Article Abstracts, or use the powerful search engine.
Registered Users are provided with a *Personal Home Page* to store and manage customized alerts, searches, and links to favorite journals and articles. Additionally, Registered Users can view free Online Sample Issues and preview selected material from major reference works.
Licensed Customers are entitled to access full-text journal articles in PDF, with select journals also offering full-text HTML.

How do I become an Authorized User?

Authorized Users are individuals authorized by a paying Customer to have access to the journals in Wiley InterScience. For example, a university that subscribes to Wiley journals is considered to be the Customer. Faculty, staff and students authorized by the university to have access to those journals in Wiley InterScience are Authorized Users. Users should contact their Library for information on which Wiley journals they have access to in Wiley InterScience.

ASK YOUR INSTITUTION ABOUT WILEY INTERSCIENCE TODAY!